2nd Deep Machine Translation Workshop (DMTW 2016)

Lisbon, Portugal
21 October 2016

ISBN: 978-1-5108-3156-8

Printed from e-media with permission by:

Curran Associates, Inc.
57 Morehouse Lane
Red Hook, NY 12571

CURRAN ASSOCIATES INC. proceedings.com

Some format issues inherent in the e-media version may also appear in this print version.

Printed by Curran Associates, Inc. (2016)

For permission requests, please contact the Association for Computational Linguistics at the address below.

Association for Computational Linguistics
209 N. Eighth Street
Stroudsburg, Pennsylvania 18360

Phone: 1-570-476-8006
Fax: 1-570-476-0860

acl@aclweb.org

Additional copies of this publication are available from:

Curran Associates, Inc.
57 Morehouse Lane
Red Hook, NY 12571 USA
Phone: 845-758-0400
Fax: 845-758-2633
Email: curran@proceedings.com
Web: www.proceedings.com

Preface

This volume contains the papers presented at DMTW-2016: Deep Machine Translation Workshop held on October 21, 2016 in Lisbon.

Each submission was reviewed by 3 program committee members. The committee decided to accept 6 papers. The submission and proceedings creation has been handled by the EasyChair system.

We thank the QTLeap EU project for providing local funding for the workshop organization, to the team of António Branoco at FCUL in Lisbon for handling local arrangements and to Rudolf Rosa for preparing the proceedings.

October 19, 2016
Lisbon, Portugal

Jan Hajič
Gertjan van Noord
António Branco

Program Committee

Jan Hajič	Charles University (Chair)
Gertjan van Noord	University of Groningen (Co-chair)
António Branco	University of Lisbon (Co-chair)
Aljoscha Burchardt	Deutsches Forschungszentrum für Künstliche Intelligenz
Deyi Xiong	Soochow University
Eneko Agirre	University of the Basque Country
Khalil Sima'an	University of Amsterdam
Kiril Simov	Bulgarian Academy of Sciences
Martin Popel	Charles University in Prague
Petya Osenova	Bulgarian Academy of Sciences
Rosa Del Gaudio	Higher Functions

Table of Contents

Moses & Treex Hybrid MT Systems Bestiary

Rudolf Rosa, Martin Popel, Ondřej Bojar, David Mareček, Ondřej Dušek
Charles University, Faculty of Mathematics and Physics,
Institute of Formal and Applied Linguistics,
Malostranské náměstí 25, 118 00 Prague, Czech Republic
{rosa,popel,bojar,marecek,odusek}@ufal.mff.cuni.cz

Abstract

Moses is a well-known representative of the phrase-based statistical machine translation systems family, which are known to be extremely poor in explicit linguistic knowledge, operating on flat language representations, consisting only of tokens and phrases. Treex, on the other hand, is a highly linguistically motivated NLP toolkit, operating on several layers of language representation, rich in linguistic annotations. Its main application is TectoMT, a hybrid machine translation system with deep syntax transfer. We review a large number of machine translation systems that have been built over the past years by combining Moses and Treex/TectoMT in various ways.

1 Introduction and Motivation

Phrase-based statistical machine translation (PB-SMT) systems, which have been the state-of-the-art approach to machine translation (MT) for many years, are known to contain very little explicit linguistic knowledge. While this characteristic has been at the core of their success, enabling fast development, training and tuning of the systems (as long as sufficient amounts of parallel data are available), it becomes a double-edged sword in many cases, e.g., when translating into a morphologically-rich language with frequent long-range dependencies, such as Czech.

It has been shown that many language phenomena hard to handle for the PB-SMT systems can be easily dealt with by linguistically motivated MT systems – although these systems often have other shortcomings, such as a tendency to translate very lexically, in a one-to-one fashion, due to lacking the (non-linguistic) phrase-based representation employed in PB-SMT systems.

This situation invites researchers to attempt to combine these conceptually different systems in a clever way so that their strengths combine and their shortcomings cancel out. In our paper, we review a set of such attempts, performed with Moses, a prominent representative of the PB-SMT systems, and Treex, a linguistically motivated NLP framework, featuring, among other, a full-fledged deep syntactic MT system, TectoMT.

As Treex and TectoMT have been primarily developed to process Czech language and to perform English-to-Czech translation, most of the existing system combination experiments have been performed on the English-to-Czech language pair.[1] Therefore, we limit ourselves to this setting in our work.

2 Individual Systems

2.1 Moses

Moses (Koehn et al., 2007) is a standard PB-SMT system. It features simple rule-based tokenization and true-casing scripts, which are sometimes language-specific, but the core of the decoder is purely statistical and oblivious of any linguistics. It relies on GIZA++ (Och and Ney, 2003) to compute word alignment of the training parallel corpus, used to extract lexicons and phrase tables that provide the knowledge of translation options to the decoder. A word-based language model is used to score possible translations, so that a fluent one can be produced as the output.

[1] A few combinations have been also applied to other translation pairs.

Proceedings of the 2nd Deep Machine Translation Workshop (DMTW 2016), pages 1–10,
Lisbon, Portugal, 21 October 2016.

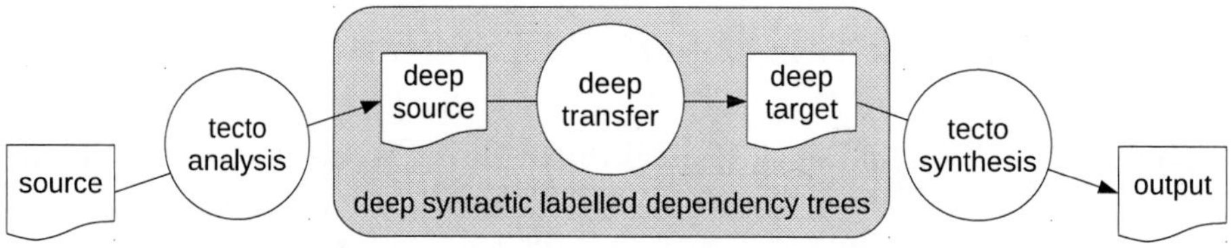

Figure 1: TectoMT

2.1.1 Factored Moses

In the more recent experiments that we report, the Moses system used is actually the Factored Moses of Bojar et al. (2012). It translates the source English text into a factored representation of Czech, where each word is represented by a tuple of a word form and a corresponding part-of-speech (PoS) tag. This enables Moses to use an additional language model which operates on PoS tags instead of word forms. This helps overcome data sparsity issues of the word-based language model and thus leads to a higher output quality, especially to its better grammaticality. Factored Moses is trained on parallel corpora pre-analyzed by Treex.

2.2 Treex

Treex[2] (Popel and Žabokrtský, 2010; Žabokrtský, 2011) is a linguistically motivated NLP framework. It consists of a large number of smaller components performing a specific NLP-task (blocks), both Treex-specific as well as Treex-wrapped external tools, which can be flexibly combined into processing pipelines. Sentences are represented by surface and deep syntactic dependency trees, richly annotated with numerous linguistic attributes, similarly to the Prague Dependency Treebank (Hajič, 1998).

2.2.1 TectoMT

The main application of Treex is TectoMT[3] (Žabokrtský et al., 2008; Dušek et al., 2015), a linguistically motivated hybrid machine translation system. Its pipieline consists of three main steps: analysis of each source sentence up to t-layer (a deep syntactic representation of the sentence in a labelled dependency t-tree), transfer of the source t-tree to the target t-tree (i.e., the translation per se), and generation of the target sentence from the target t-tree (see Figure 1).

The transfer is performed by copying the t-tree structure and *grammatemes*[4] (attributes describing grammatical meaning) from source, and predicting target lemmas and *formemes*[5] (deep morphosyntactic attributes (Dušek et al., 2012)) using a set of machine-learned translation models. In the current transfer implementation, TectoMT translates t-tree nodes one-to-one; however, as function words are abstracted from, a one-to-one correspondence between t-trees in different languages is present in most cases.

3 System Combinations

This section contains description and evaluation of several system combination setups. We list a number of combinations of Moses and Treex/TectoMT that we are aware of, both successful and unsuccessful.

Results of automatic evaluation of the setups, as reported in available literature,[6] are provided in Table 1. We report absolute *differences* in BLEU scores[7] versus the base systems, rather than the absolute scores themselves – the setups were evaluated on many different test sets, and it is well known that BLEU scores are not directly comparable across datasets. Still, for each of the references in Table 1, we also list the absolute scores of the base system(s) in Table 2. We round up the scores to one decimal digit.

[2] http://ufal.mff.cuni.cz/treex

[3] http://ufal.mff.cuni.cz/tectomt

[4] https://ufal.mff.cuni.cz/pdt2.0/doc/manuals/en/t-layer/html/ch05s05.html

[5] https://ufal.mff.cuni.cz/pcedt2.0/en/formemes.html

[6] Except for "Moses + TectoMT post-editing" (Section 3.4), which we ran and evaluated ourselves.

[7] The scores are either case-sensitive or case-insensitive BLEU scores, depending on what was reported in the referenced paper. We do not include information on statistical significance of the score differences, as most of the authors did not report that. We kindly ask the interested reader to refer directly to the referenced papers or to their authors for any further details.

	Setup	Δ BLEU versus base Moses	TectoMT	Reference
§ 3.1	TectoMoses: TectoMT with Moses transfer		−2.2	Popel (2015)
§ 3.2	PhraseFix: TectoMT + Moses post-editing		+2.7	Bojar et al. (2013a)
			+3.2	Galuščáková et al. (2013)
§ 3.3	Moses + Moses post-editing, simple	−0.1		Rosa (2013)
	Moses + Moses post-editing, TwoStep	−0.1		Bojar and Kos (2010)
§ 3.4	Google Translate + TectoMT post-editing	*−0.9		Majliš (2009)
	Moses + TectoMT post-editing	−2.4	+2.4	Section 3.4 & Bojar et al. (2016)
§ 3.5	Moses + Depfix post-editing	+0.1		Mareček et al. (2011)
		+0.1		Rosa et al. (2012)
		+0.4		Rosa (2013)
§ 3.6	Joshua + Treex pre-processing	**+0.5		Zeman (2010)
	Moses + Treex pre-/post-processing	+0.4		Rosa et al. (2016)
§ 3.7	Two-headed Chimera: Moses + TectoMT		+4.7	Bojar et al. (2013a)
		+0.6	+5.4	Bojar et al. (2013b)
			+5.5	Bojar et al. (2014)
		+1.1	+5.3	Bojar et al. (2015)
		+1.6		Bojar and Tamchyna (2015)
		+1.3	+6.1	Bojar et al. (2016)
§ 3.8	Chimera: Moses + TectoMT + Depfix		+5.0	Bojar et al. (2013a)
		+0.5	+5.3	Bojar et al. (2013b)
			+5.7	Bojar et al. (2014)
		+1.2	+5.4	Bojar et al. (2015)
		+1.5	+6.3	Bojar et al. (2016)
		+1.1		Tamchyna et al. (2016)

Table 1: System combinations. Difference in BLEU versus the Moses and/or TectoMT base system; * versus Google Translate, ** versus Joshua.

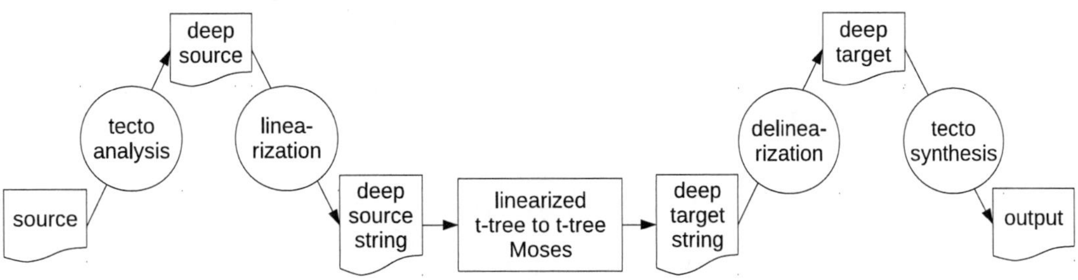

Figure 2: TectoMoses: TectoMT with Moses Transfer

While most of the setups have been properly described and evaluated in a peer-reviewed publication, others, especially some of the unsuccessful ones, were never properly published; in such cases, the descriptions and results are based on semi-official materials provided by the authors of the experiments.

3.1 TectoMoses: TectoMT with Moses Transfer

In the TectoMoses experiment of Popel (2013), which is depicted in Figure 2, the transfer step of TectoMT is substituted with Moses. This means that after the analysis to t-layer, each source-language t-tree is linearized into a sequence of lemmas and formemes (either as two factors, or interleaved). This linearized sequence is translated by Moses (trained on such data) into a target-language sequence of lemmas and formemes. Afterwards, dependencies are projected (using Moses alignment) from the source t-tree to the target sequence to reconstruct the target t-tree. Grammatemes and other attributes are also projected along the alignment. Finally, target-language synthesis is performed (as usual in TectoMT).

TectoMT's main transfer is isomorphic, which means translating one t-node to one t-node and keeping the dependency structure of the t-tree unchanged. This is much more powerful that surface word-to-word translation because t-nodes can represent e.g. complex verb forms ("*have been done*" is translated as "*bylo uděláno*"). However, there are still many cases which cannot be translated isomorphically on the t-layer. One of the advantages of TectoMoses is that it allows non-isomorphic transfer on t-layer, e.g.

System	BLEU	Reference
TectoMT	14.2	Bojar et al. (2013a)
	14.7	Bojar et al. (2013b)
	14.7	Galuščáková et al. (2013)
	15.4	Bojar et al. (2014)
	13.9	Bojar et al. (2015)
	12.4	Popel (2015)
	14.7	Bojar et al. (2016)
Moses	14.2	Bojar and Kos (2010)
	16.0	Mareček et al. (2011)
	15.4	Rosa et al. (2012)
	16.4	Rosa (2013)
	19.5	Bojar et al. (2013b)
	17.6	Bojar et al. (2015)
	22.6	Bojar and Tamchyna (2015)
	19.5	Bojar et al. (2016)
	19.1	Tamchyna et al. (2016)
	23.3	Rosa et al. (2016)
Google Translate	5.3	Majliš (2009)
Joshua	8.6	Zeman (2010)

Table 2: Base systems.

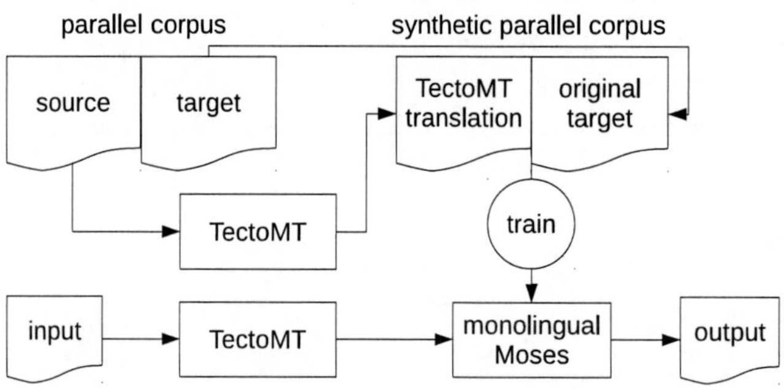

Figure 3: PhraseFix

translating one t-node with two or more t-nodes or deleting some t-nodes.[8] It also uses MERT tuning and it should scale with more training data. In the experiments with two factors (Popel, 2013), two language models were used: one for lemmas and one for formemes. Unfortunately, the TectoMoses experiment brought negative results, presumably due to additional noise introduced by the added transformations.

3.2 PhraseFix: TectoMT with Moses Post-editing

The PhraseFix system of Galuščáková et al. (2013) is based on the work of Simard et al. (2007), who introduced the idea of automatically post-editing a first-stage MT system by a second-stage MT system, trained to "translate" the output of the first-stage system into a reference translation. This has been shown to be particularly beneficial for conceptually different MT systems. In PhraseFix, the source English side of the CzEng parallel corpus of Bojar and Žabokrtský (2009) is translated by TectoMT into Czech, and Moses is then trained in a monolingual setting to translate the TectoMT-Czech into reference-Czech, i.e., the target side of CzEng (see Figure 3). Evaluation shows that this approach works well in principle, significantly improving the quality of the output as compared to the base TectoMT system. However, it does not surpass the translation quality provided by a standard standalone bilingual Moses.

3.3 Moses with Moses Post-editing

In case one does not have two different systems to combine, the simple approach of Oflazer and El-Kahlout (2007) can always be tried, who were the first to report translation quality improvements by

[8] PhraseFix (Section 3.2) also allows non-isomorphic translation, but only as post-processing. All other Moses-based systems (including Chimera, Section 3.7 & Section 3.8) allow non-isomorphic translations, but their transfer is on the t-layer.

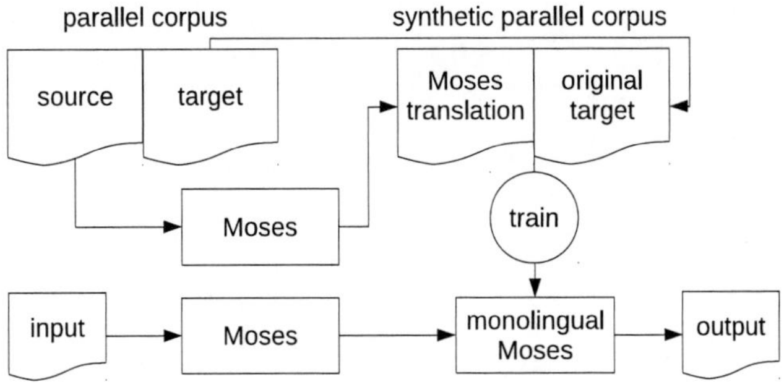

Figure 4: Simple post-editing of Moses by Moses

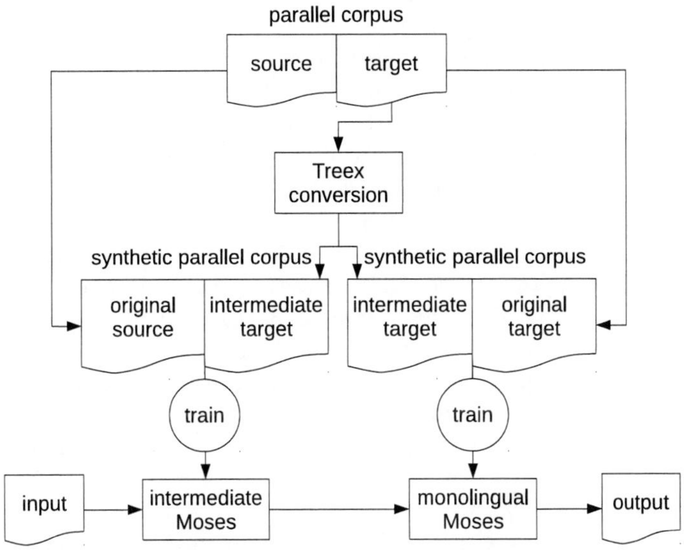

Figure 5: TwoStep Moses translation

training Moses to post-edit its own output. The setup, shown in Figure 4, is generally identical to that described in Section 3.2, except for using a standard bilingual Moses as the first-stage system, and then again Moses, this time in a monolingual setting, as the second-stage system. This setup was implemented and evaluated for English-to-Czech translation in (Rosa, 2013, section 7.4.1), but no improvements were found; based on a review of previous papers reporting positive results, the authors noted that this approach is probably only useful in cases where the available parallel training corpus is very small.

A more elaborate attempt in the same direction was presented as the TwoStep setup of Bojar and Kos (2010), this time bringing in Treex as well. TwoStep uses a first-stage Moses to translate from English into *intermediate Czech*, where each word is represented by a tuple of its lemma and a label marking several morphological features (such as detailed PoS, morphological number, grade, and negation). The second-stage Moses then translates from intermediate Czech into Czech (see Figure 5). The conversion of Czech into intermediate Czech is performed by a Treex pipeline described by Bojar and Žabokrtský (2009), with the main component being the Morče tagger of Spoustová et al. (2007). Unfortunately, this complex setup has not been found to have any benefit either.

3.4 Moses with TectoMT Post-editing

This setup uses Moses with transfer-less TectoMT as a post-editing tool (see Figure 6). A transfer-less TectoMT performs a tecto-analysis of the input, and then immediately proceeds with the tecto-synthesis

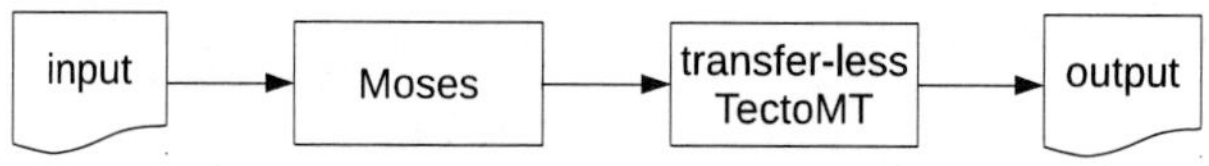

Figure 6: Moses with TectoMT post-editing

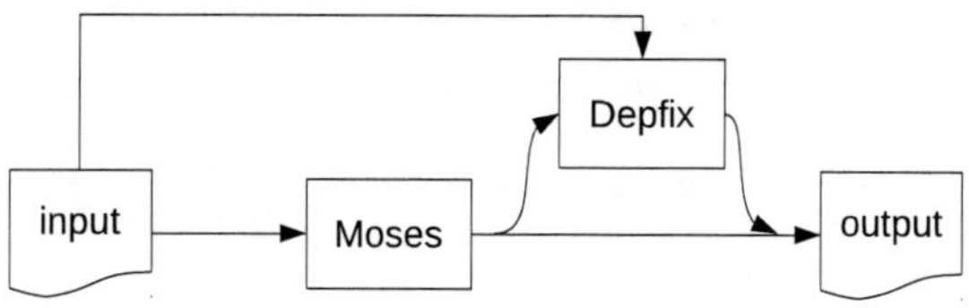

Figure 7: Moses with Depfix post-editing

of the output, completely omitting the interlingual transfer step.

Theoretically, analysis and a subsequent synthesis of a correct sentence should lead to the output being identical to the input (except for real synonymy). The motivation of Moses with transfer-less TectoMT post-editing was that incorrect sentences should be fixed this way, especially with respect to grammatical agreement. However, even the first assumption of identical output for correct sentences is not always true in practice, as some of the Treex blocks are not 100% accurate. Unfortunately, the assumption about fixing incorrect sentences also did not stand the practical test, mainly because the incorrect sentence on input tends to confuse the analysis pipeline and often leads to a largely incorrect analysis being produced (even if we disregard the fact that it is hard to define a correct analysis of an incorrect sentence).

We have been unable to find any work evaluating this particular setup, apart from the project of Majliš (2009), who applied TectoMT post-editing to Google Translate.[9] Therefore, we rerun the experiment ourselves, using current TectoMT[10] to post-edit the output of Moses obtained from the website of the WMT 2016 translation task (Bojar et al., 2016),[11] confirming the negative result reported by Majliš.

3.5 Moses with Depfix Post-editing

Similarly to the previous setup, Moses is complemented by a post-editing system implemented in Treex; this time, the system is Depfix (see Figure 7). Depfix (Mareček et al., 2011; Rosa, 2014) consists of several dozens rule-based post-editing Treex blocks. It focuses mainly on enforcing grammatical correctness, e.g., marking the subject and object by inflectional endings based on analysis of the source sentence, or inflecting adjectives to morphologically agree with their head nouns in gender, number, and case. However, contrary to the TectoMT post-editing (Section 3.4), it only modifies the erroneous parts of the output, thus avoiding generating too much noise; its second strength is the availability of the source analysis to the post-editing blocks, which enables them to make better-informed decisions regarding the intended meaning of the target sentence. This leads to a small but consistent improvement in BLEU.

3.6 Moses with Treex Pre- and Post-processing

Here, Treex is used in a more aggressive way, modifying the input and/or output to account for phenomena that the PB-SMT system is known not to be able to handle well (see Figure 8).

[9] `https://translate.google.com/`

[10] The 13th September 2016 version of the Treex repository, `https://github.com/ufal/treex/`

[11] `cu-plain` Moses output downloaded from `http://matrix.statmt.org/systems/show/2807`, test set downloaded from `http://matrix.statmt.org/test_sets/list`.

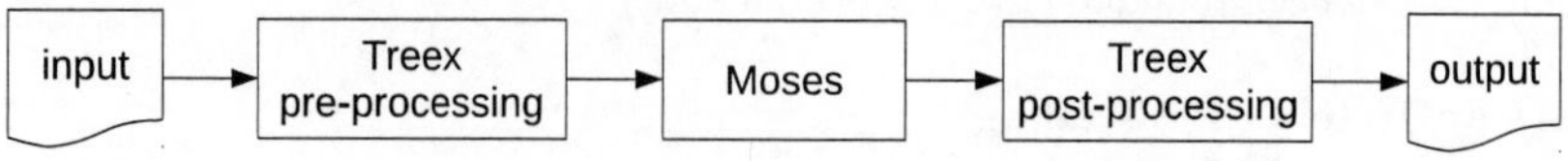

Figure 8: Moses with TectoMT pre- and post-processing

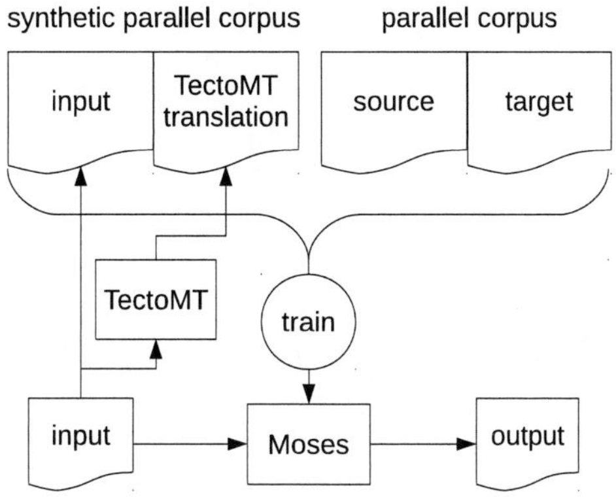

Figure 9: Two-headed Chimera

Zeman (2010) used several pre-processing steps to make the source English text more similar to Czech, such as removing articles, marking subjects by artificial suffixes ("/Sb"), and reordering auxiliary verbs to neighbor their main verbs. Of course, the SMT system was also trained on texts preprocessed in that way; in these experiments, the Joshua PB-SMT system (Li et al., 2009) was used instead of Moses. This approach may seem too aggressive, prone to making the input noisier as well as being potentially lossy. However, the author showed that with careful selection and tuning of the pre-processing steps, a significant improvement of translation quality can be achieved; moreover, this was also confirmed on English-to-Hindi translation.

Rosa et al. (2016) successfully apply Treex pre-processing and post-processing to Moses, but this time with the main objective being an adaptation of Moses trained on general-domain data to a specific domain (namely the domain of Information Technology). The authors use Treex to perform *forced translation* of identified named entities, using a named entity recognizer and a bilingual gazetteer, as well as *forced non-translation* of special structures (URLs, e-mail addresses, computer commands and filenames); Moses XML annotation is used to preserve the forcedly translated items.[12] Apart from domain adaptation, simpler general Treex pre- and post-processing steps were also successfully used, such as projection of letter case in identical words from source to target.

3.7 Two-headed Chimera: Moses with Additional TectoMT Phrase-table

The Two-headed Chimera or AddToTrain (Bojar et al., 2013b; Bojar and Tamchyna, 2015)is a combination of full TectoMT with full Moses (see Figure 9). First, the input is translated by TectoMT. TectoMT translations are then joined with the input to create a small synthetic parallel corpus, from which a secondary phrase table is extracted. This is then used together with the primary phrase table, extracted from the large training data, to train Moses. Finally, the input is translated by the resulting Moses system.

This setup enables Moses to use parts of the TectoMT translation that it considers good, while still having the base large phrase table at its disposal. This has been shown to have a positive effect, e.g., in choosing the correct inflection of a word when the language model encounters an unknown context, or in generating a translation for a word that constitutes an out-of-vocabulary item for Moses (as TectoMT can abstract from word forms to lemmas and beyond, which Moses cannot).

3.8 Chimera: Moses with Additional TectoMT Phrase-table and Depfix Post-editing

The Three-headed Chimera, or simply Chimera (Bojar et al., 2013b; Tamchyna et al., 2016), is a combination of TectoMT and Moses, as in Section 3.7, complemented by a final post-editing step performed by Depfix, as in Section 3.5 (see Figure 10). It has been repeatedly confirmed as the best system by both automatic and manual evaluations, not only among the ones reported in this paper, but also in general,

[12]`http://www.statmt.org/moses/?n=Advanced.Hybrid`

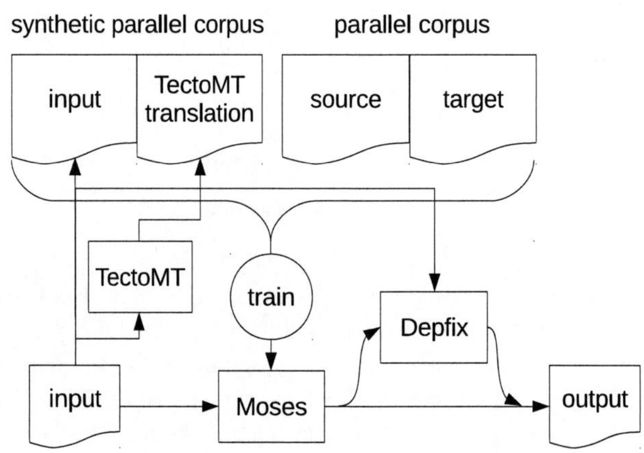

Figure 10: Three-headed Chimera

being the winner of the WMT English-to-Czech translation task in the years 2013, 2014 and 2015 (Bojar et al., 2013a; Bojar et al., 2014; Bojar et al., 2015).

4 Conclusion

We reviewed a range of existing methods of combining the linguistically poor Moses phrase-based machine translation system with linguistically rich systems implemented in the Treex NLP framework, most notably the TectoMT system, including their automatic evaluation via BLEU as reported in the literature. Some of the methods have been shown to achieve significant improvements in the translation quality, as measured by BLEU as well as by human evaluation. The most successful are the Chimera methods, which constituted the state-of-the-art in English-to-Czech machine translation in several WMT translation shared tasks.

On the other hand, many other methods have not brought any significant improvement, or have even lead to a deterioration of the translation quality. However, we believe these methods to be worth considering as well, as they bring more insight into the problematics of hybrid translation. Moreover, some of them might be further modified or combined in future, and may eventually become useful, possibly for a different language pair or for a specific domain.

Acknowledgements

This research was supported by the grants FP7-ICT-2013-10-610516 (QTLeap), GAUK 1572314, GAUK 2058214, and SVV 260 333. This work has been using language resources and tools developed, stored and distributed by the LINDAT/CLARIN project of the Ministry of Education, Youth and Sports of the Czech Republic (project LM2015071).

References

Ondřej Bojar and Kamil Kos. 2010. 2010 failures in English-Czech phrase-based MT. In *Proceedings of the Joint Fifth WMT and MetricsMATR*, pages 60–66, Uppsala, Sweden. Uppsala Universitet, ACL.

Ondřej Bojar and Aleš Tamchyna. 2015. CUNI in WMT15: Chimera strikes again. In *Proceedings of the 10th WMT*, pages 79–83, Stroudsburg, PA, USA. ACL.

Ondřej Bojar and Zdeněk Žabokrtský. 2009. CzEng 0.9, building a large Czech-English automatic parallel treebank. *PBML*, (92):63–83.

Ondřej Bojar, Bushra Jawaid, and Amir Kamran. 2012. Probes in a taxonomy of factored phrase-based models. In *Proceedings of the Seventh WMT*, pages 253–260, Montréal, Canada. ACL.

Ondřej Bojar, Christian Buck, Chris Callison-Burch, Christian Federmann, Barry Haddow, Philipp Koehn, Christof Monz, Matt Post, Radu Soricut, and Lucia Specia. 2013a. Findings of the 2013 WMT. In *Proceedings of the Eight WMT*, pages 1–44, Sofija, Bulgaria. Bălgarska akademija na naukite, ACL.

Ondřej Bojar, Rudolf Rosa, and Aleš Tamchyna. 2013b. Chimera – three heads for English-to-Czech translation. In *Proceedings of the Eight WMT*, pages 92–98, Sofija, Bulgaria. Bălgarska akademija na naukite, ACL.

Ondřej Bojar, Christian Buck, Christian Federmann, Barry Haddow, Philipp Koehn, Johannes Leveling, Christof Monz, Pavel Pecina, Matt Post, Herve Saint-Amand, Radu Soricut, Lucia Specia, and Aleš Tamchyna. 2014. Findings of the 2014 WMT. In *Proceedings of the Ninth WMT*, pages 12–58, Baltimore, MD, USA. ACL.

Ondřej Bojar, Rajen Chatterjee, Christian Federmann, Barry Haddow, Matthias Huck, Chris Hokamp, Philipp Koehn, Varvara Logacheva, Christof Monz, Matteo Negri, Matt Post, Carolina Scarton, Lucia Specia, and Marco Turchi. 2015. Findings of the 2015 WMT. In *Proceedings of the 10th WMT*, pages 1–46, Stroudsburg, PA, USA. ACL.

Ondřej Bojar, Rajen Chatterjee, Christian Federmann, Yvette Graham, Barry Haddow, Matthias Huck, Antonio Yepes, Philipp Koehn, Varvara Logacheva, Christof Monz, Matteo Negri, Aurelie Névéol, Mariana Neves, Martin Popel, Matt Post, Raphael Rubino, Carolina Scarton, Lucia Specia, Marco Turchi, Karin Verspoor, and Marcos Zampieri. 2016. Findings of the 2016 conference on machine translation (WMT16). In Ondřej Bojar and et al ., editors, *Proceedings of the First Conference on Machine Translation (WMT). Volume 2: Shared Task Papers*, volume 2, pages 131–198, Stroudsburg, PA, USA. ACL.

Ondřej Dušek, Luís Gomes, Michal Novák, Martin Popel, and Rudolf Rosa. 2015. New language pairs in TectoMT. In *Proceedings of the 10th WMT*, pages 98–104, Stroudsburg, PA, USA. ACL.

Ondřej Dušek, Zdeněk Žabokrtský, Martin Popel, Martin Majliš, Michal Novák, and David Mareček. 2012. Formemes in English-Czech deep syntactic MT. In *Proceedings of the Seventh WMT*, page 267–274.

Petra Galuščáková, Martin Popel, and Ondřej Bojar. 2013. PhraseFix: Statistical post-editing of tectoMT. In *Proceedings of the Eight WMT*, pages 141–147, Sofija, Bulgaria. Bălgarska akademija na naukite, ACL.

Jan Hajič. 1998. Building a Syntactically Annotated Corpus: The Prague Dependency Treebank. In Eva Hajičová, editor, *Issues of Valency and Meaning. Studies in Honor of Jarmila Panevová*, pages 12–19. Prague Karolinum, Charles University Press.

Philipp Koehn, Hieu Hoang, Alexandra Birch, Chris Callison-Burch, Marcello Federico, Nicola Bertoldi, Brooke Cowan, Wade Shen, Christine Moran, Richard Zens, Chris Dyer, Ondřej Bojar, Alexandra Constantin, and Evan Herbst. 2007. Moses: Open source toolkit for statistical machine translation. In *ACL 2007, Proceedings of the 45th Annual Meeting of the ACL Companion Volume Proceedings of the Demo and Poster Sessions*, pages 177–180, Prague, Czech Republic, June. ACL.

Zhifei Li, Chris Callison-Burch, Sanjeev Khudanpur, and Wren Thornton. 2009. Decoding in Joshua: Open source, parsing-based machine translation. *PBML*, 91:47–56.

Martin Majliš. 2009. Google Translate + TectoMT. `http://www.slideshare.net/martin.majlis/google-translate-tectomt`, May. Oral talk.

David Mareček, Rudolf Rosa, Petra Galuščáková, and Ondřej Bojar. 2011. Two-step translation with grammatical post-processing. In Chris Callison-Burch, Philipp Koehn, Christof Monz, and Omar Zaidan, editors, *Proceedings of the Sixth WMT*, pages 426–432, Edinburgh, UK. University of Edinburgh, ACL.

Franz Josef Och and Hermann Ney. 2003. A systematic comparison of various statistical alignment models. *Computational Linguistics*, 29(1):19–51.

Kemail Oflazer and Ilknur Durgar El-Kahlout. 2007. Exploring different representational units in English-to-Turkish statistical machine translation. In *Proceedings of the Second WMT*, pages 25–32. ACL.

Martin Popel and Zdeněk Žabokrtský. 2010. TectoMT: Modular NLP framework. In Hrafn Loftsson, Eirikur Rögnvaldsson, and Sigrun Helgadottir, editors, *LNAI, Proceedings of the 7th International Conference on Advances in NLP (IceTAL 2010)*, volume 6233 of *LNCS*, pages 293–304, Berlin / Heidelberg. Iceland Centre for Language Technology (ICLT), Springer.

Martin Popel. 2013. Machine translation zoo: Tree-to-tree transfer and discriminative learning. `https://ufal.mff.cuni.cz/~popel/papers/2013_05_06_zoo.pdf`, May. Oral talk.

Martin Popel. 2015. Machine translation and discriminative models: Tree-to-tree transfer and discriminative learning. `http://ufal.mff.cuni.cz/~popel/papers/2015_03_23_discriminative_tectomt.pdf`, March. Oral talk.

Rudolf Rosa, David Mareček, and Ondřej Dušek. 2012. DEPFIX: A system for automatic correction of Czech MT outputs. In *Proceedings of the Seventh WMT*, pages 362–368, Montréal, Canada. ACL.

Rudolf Rosa, Roman Sudarikov, Michal Novák, Martin Popel, and Ondřej Bojar. 2016. Dictionary-based domain adaptation of MT systems without retraining. In Ondřej Bojar and et al ., editors, *Proceedings of the First Conference on Machine Translation (WMT). Volume 2: Shared Task Papers*, volume 2, pages 449–455, Stroudsburg, PA, USA. ACL.

Rudolf Rosa. 2013. Automatic post-editing of phrase-based machine translation outputs. Master's thesis, Charles University in Prague, Faculty of Mathematics and Physics, Praha, Czechia.

Rudolf Rosa. 2014. Depfix, a tool for automatic rule-based post-editing of SMT. *PBML*, 102:47–56.

Michel Simard, Cyril Goutte, and Pierre Isabelle. 2007. Statistical phrase-based post-editing. In *HLT 2007: The Conference of the North American Chapter of the ACL; Proceedings of the Main Conference*, pages 508–515, Rochester, New York, April. ACL.

Drahomíra Spoustová, Jan Hajič, Jan Votrubec, Pavel Krbec, and Pavel Květoň. 2007. The best of two worlds: Cooperation of statistical and rule-based taggers for Czech. In *Proceedings of the Workshop on Balto-Slavonic NLP 2007*, pages 67–74, Praha, Czechia. Univerzita Karlova v Praze, ACL.

Aleš Tamchyna, Roman Sudarikov, Ondřej Bojar, and Alexander Fraser. 2016. CUNI-LMU submissions in WMT2016: Chimera constrained and beaten. In Ondřej Bojar and et al ., editors, *Proceedings of the First Conference on Machine Translation (WMT). Volume 2: Shared Task Papers*, volume 2, pages 385–390, Stroudsburg, PA, USA. ACL, ACL.

Zdeněk Žabokrtský. 2011. Treex – an open-source framework for natural language processing. In Markéta Lopatková, editor, *Information Technologies – Applications and Theory*, volume 788, pages 7–14, Košice, Slovakia. Univerzita Pavla Jozefa Šafárika v Košiciach.

Zdeněk Žabokrtský, Jan Ptáček, and Petr Pajas. 2008. TectoMT: highly modular MT system with tectogrammatics used as transfer layer. In *Proceedings of the Third WMT*, pages 167–170. ACL.

Daniel Zeman. 2010. Using TectoMT as a preprocessing tool for phrase-based statistical machine translation. In Petr Sojka, Aleš Horák, Ivan Kopeček, and Karel Pala, editors, *Text, Speech and Dialogue*, volume 6231 of *LNCS*, pages 216–223, Berlin / Heidelberg. Masarykova univerzita, Springer.

Factoring Adjunction in Hierarchical Phrase-Based SMT

Sophie Arnoult
ILLC
University of Amsterdam
`s.i.arnoult@uva.nl`

Khalil Sima'an
ILLC
University of Amsterdam
`k.simaan@uva.nl`

Abstract

While much work has been done to inform Hierarchical Phrase-Based SMT (Chiang, 2005) models linguistically, the adjunct/argument distinction has generally not been exploited for these models. But as Shieber (2007) points out, capturing this distinction allows to abstract over 'intervening' adjuncts, and is thus relevant for (machine) translation in general. We contribute an adjunction-driven approach to hierarchical phrase-based modelling that uses source-side adjuncts to relax extraction constraints–allowing to capturing long-distance dependencies–, and to guide translation through labelling. The labelling scheme can be reduced to two adjunct/non-adjunct labels, and improves translation over Hiero by up to 0.6 BLEU points for English-Chinese.

1 Introduction

Hiero (Chiang, 2005) extends phrase-based Statistical Machine Translation models (Koehn et al., 2003) by allowing phrase pairs to rewrite through a Synchronous CFG mechanism. Rewriting is unconstrained, and the model thus learns local dependencies and reorderings in a very general manner. This lack of restrictions allows the grammar to achieve good coverage, but begs the question of how to guide Hiero with linguistic information. Since SAMT (Zollmann and Venugopal, 2006), a branch of work has focused on labelling Hiero, with different types of labels: phrase-structure labels (Zollmann and Venugopal, 2006), dependency head labels (Li et al., 2012), CCG labels (Almaghout et al., 2011), (non-syntactic) hierarchical alignment labels (Maillette de Buy Wenniger and Sima'an, 2013), etc. Most of these models use large nonterminal vocabularies, as syntactic labels or POS tags are combined into phrase labels.

The general character of Hiero is balanced by constraints on the extraction and the form of rules, and another branch of work has focused on rebalancing such constraints. For instance, Li et al. (2013) constrain rewriting to constituents or sequences of constituents, allowing them to relax phrase length at extraction. Perhaps the most obvious limitation of Hiero is its limited capacity to capture sentence-level reordering, as it can only monotonically concatenate larger fragments. This has motivated work on reordering, e.g., (Mylonakis and Sima'an, 2011; Huck et al., 2012).

We propose to extend the scope of rule extraction in Hiero around adjuncts. As adjunction introduces long-distance dependencies, allowing the extraction of larger phrases that contain adjuncts should lead to phrases that still capture useful dependencies. This is akin to the linguistic motivation for Tree-Adjoining Grammar (Joshi et al., 1975), where factoring recursion allows to keep dependencies local (Joshi and Schabes, 1997). Our model relaxes length constraints for phrase extraction by discounting the length of adjuncts contained in a phrase. This allows to learn phrases that Hiero may not learn, such as in the example of Figure 1. Ignoring intervening adjuncts at phrase extraction reduces the apparent length of the source sentence, allowing for its extraction under the standard Hiero phrase-length constraint. As the adjuncts in this example introduce a complex phrase permutation, our model is able to extract rules from this phrase, that cannot otherwise be rendered with Hiero and monotonic glue rules. Besides, we inform the model by labelling adjuncts and non-adjuncts separately. While adjuncts form only a fraction of the

Proceedings of the 2nd Deep Machine Translation Workshop (DMTW 2016), pages 11–20,
Lisbon, Portugal, 21 October 2016.

Figure 1: Example sentence; adjuncts cause long-distance dependencies (10 tokens separate 'workers' from 'have' in the English sentence) and complex reorderings (adjunction introduces a 2-4-1-3 permutation).

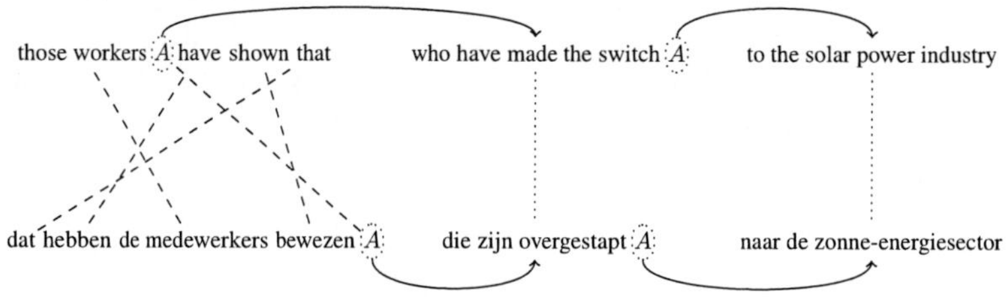

phrase pairs that can be extracted by Hiero, we find that this labelling is useful, allowing to gain up to 0.6 BLEU points on English-Chinese combined with a basic feature set.

Factoring adjunction also allows to learn more general rules. DeNeefe and Knight (2009) show this improves translation for syntax-based models. We propose to extend the Hiero grammar by excising adjuncts from extraction phrases. This is similar in spirit to the approach of (Arnoult and Sima'an, 2012) for phrase-based models, but with the added capacity to extract SCFG rules from modified phrases. In our example, this allows to extract rules from the (adjunct-free) phrase "those workers have shown that"/"dat hebben de medewerkers bewezen".

The rest of this article is organized as follows: section 2 deals with adjunction, and how we identify it; section 3 presents our extensions to Hiero; section 4 presents experiments on three language pairs, with English as source language, and Chinese, Dutch and French as target languages; we discuss the results of these experiments in section 5 and conclude in section 6.

2 Identifying adjuncts

Adjunction in Tree-Adjoining Grammar allows to explain a number of linguistic phenomena like raising or wh movement (Kroch and Joshi, 1985), but we focus here on modification, which we identify with dependency labels (we use the Turbo parser[1]).

We identify modifier labels and punctuation with adjuncts: `AMOD`, `NMOD`, `VMOD` and `P`. We exclude cases where the dependent appears obligatory, based on the head's POS tag: `DT`, `EX`, `IN`, `POS`, `MD`, `PRP`, `PRP$`, `RP`, `SYM`, `TO`, `WDT`, `WP`, `WP$`, `WRB`, `.`; we also exclude possessors in genitive constructions, by excluding dependents preceding a dependent with a `POS` part of speech.

We include dependents of enumerations and conjunctions in the list of modifiers. This follows from a dependency analysis that treats one of the conjuncts as the head, and conjunctions and other conjuncts as its dependents. In the case of the Turbo parser, the last conjunct or element in an enumeration is regarded as the head. We modified this representation to a nested one, where conjunctions are treated as heads of the dependent conjunct, as shown in Figure 2.

Figure 2: Modifying the representation of enumerations and conjunctions. Dotted lines represent non adjuncts.

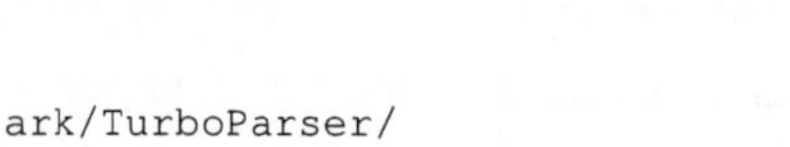

[1] `http://www.cs.cmu.edu/~ark/TurboParser/`

3 Model

We present an adjunction-driven extension to Hiero with two distinguishing features: we use adjuncts to guide the extraction from larger phrases than normally allowed by Hiero; and we apply labelling to let the model distinguish adjuncts from arguments and other phrases. We present the extraction constraints in section 3.1, the labelling method in section 3.2, and the features we use for the model in section 3.3. Additionally, section 3.4 presents another extension, inspired from (Arnoult and Sima'an, 2012), that leverages adjunct optionality to extract additional rules.

3.1 Adjunction-driven extraction constraints

Hiero limits phrase spans for rule extraction through a *max-phrase-length* constraint (of typically 10 tokens). This limit is needed to restrict the number of extractable phrases, that may grow exponentially with sentence length. Further, reorderings may manifest themselves differently locally than at the sentence level, so that the task of learning sentence-level rules may be better handled separately. However, as adjunction introduces long-distance dependencies, factoring it out should allow to extract more relevant phrase pairs.

We use adjunction as a guide to extending rule extraction for larger phrases. Like Hiero, we allow extraction and unconstrained rewriting of all phrases under *max-phrase-length.* For larger phrases, we subject extraction and rewriting to three constraints: *max-effective-length*, *non-adjunct-crossing*, and *max-target-symbols.* Besides, we apply specific constraints to adjuncts and adjunct sequences.

max-effective-length

We define the effective length as the non-adjunct token count of phrase. Let a phrase ϕ, that contains $\alpha_0..\alpha_n$ adjuncts (disregarding adjuncts embedded in other adjuncts), its effective length $\lambda(\phi)$ is:

$$\lambda(\phi) = \text{len}(\phi) - \Sigma_{i=0}^{n}\text{len}(\alpha_i)$$

In practice, we set *max-effective-length* to the same value as *max-phrase-length.*

This constraint only applies to non-adjunct phrases, as we allow the extraction of all phrases that match an adjunct on the source side, or a group of adjuncts: we group together adjuncts that have the same orientation with regard to their head, and that form contiguous sequences on source and target sides.

no-adjunct-crossing

This constraint prevents the extraction of larger phrases that cross adjuncts, or groups of adjuncts. This forces rewriting to an adjunct group as a whole. When rewriting from an adjunct group, one only forbids adjunct crossings, allowing rewriting to sub-groups.

max-target-symbols

Hiero limits the number of right-hand-side symbols on the rules' source sides. The length of the target side can also be limited: for Hiero, we apply *max-phrase-length* to the target side of extraction phrase pairs; for the adjunction-based models, we limit the number of target right-hand-side symbols to the same value as *max-phrase-length.*

Table 1 shows a possible derivation for the example of Figure 1. Allowing the extraction of rules from larger phrases permits to capture long-range dependencies and reorderings inaccessible to Hiero. While rule r_1 is likely in fact to be learnt by Hiero in a different context, rule r_2 displays a pattern (extraposed modifier in the Dutch sentence but not in the English sentence) that is only likely to occur with a long modifier.

3.2 Labelling

To further guide the model, we apply labelling to distinguish adjuncts from other phrases. We identify source adjuncts and adjunct sequences, and label both sides of rules and rule gaps accordingly: with an A label for adjuncts; an Ax label for adjunct groups of size x; and a default label for other phrases.

Table 1: Example rules for the example in Figure 1

r_1	X $\rightarrow$ ⟨ X that , dat X ⟩
r_2	X $\rightarrow$ ⟨ those workers $A^{[1]}$ have shown , hebben de medewerkers bewezen $A^{[1]}$ ⟩
r_3	A $\rightarrow$ ⟨ $X^{[1]}$ made the switch $A^{[2]}$, $X^{[1]}$ overgestapt $A^{[2]}$⟩
r_4	X $\rightarrow$ ⟨ who have , die zijn ⟩
r_5	A $\rightarrow$ ⟨ to the solar power industry , naar de zonne-energiesector ⟩

3.3 Features

The model uses two rule features to distinguish larger phrase pairs from Hiero-extractable phrase pairs: a *long-distance* feature, corresponding to the probability estimate that a rule was extracted from a larger phrase pair (exceeding Hiero's *max-phrase-length*); and an *adjunct-crossing* feature corresponding to the probability that a rule was extracted from a (shorter) phrase pair violating the *non-adjunct-crossing* constraint.

Besides, we tested a version of the model with a simplified labelling for adjunct sequences. These sequences are then labelled with A instead of Ax, while their size x appears in the following feature:

$$f_x = e^{1-x} \tag{1}$$

For other rules (adjuncts and other phrase pairs), f_x is taken to be 1.

3.4 Factoring out adjuncts

TAG factors adjunction by extracting auxiliary trees and initial trees separately (Joshi and Schabes, 1997). This leads to a more compact grammar (Chiang, 2000) that is able to generate unseen adjunction patterns. Synchronous Tree Adjunction Grammar (STAG) (Shieber and Schabes, 1990) applies TAG to translation, and DeNeefe and Knight (2009) propose a probabilistic implementation for string-to-tree translation. Their model identifies target-side adjuncts and takes their projection on the source side as a basis for auxilliary-tree extraction.

In the case of Hiero, one cannot directly implement STAG, as CFG rules do not have the (tree) structure that is necessary for modelling adjunction. One can still however extract generalized versions of rules, by factoring out adjuncts contained in extraction phrases. This follows (Arnoult and Sima'an, 2012), who apply this idea to a phrase-based model. The hierarchical nature of Hiero further allows to apply substitution in these generalized phrases.

We extend Hiero by extracting rules both by standard phrase substitution, and by adjunct factorization. For each phrase pair in the training data, we first extract rules by substitution. For each adjunct contained in the phrase pair, we instantiate a copy of the extraction phrase where the adjunct is *blind*: the adjunct blocks the extraction of overlapping gaps, and its yield is excised from the rule. We then extract rules by phrase substitution from this extraction phrase; Table 2 shows some of the resulting rules for the example of Figure 1. The rules extracted in this manner form a subset of the rules that Hiero would extract from the phrase pair ⟨ those workers have shown, hebben de medewerkers bewezen ⟩, as we forbid gaps from overlapping with blind adjuncts.

Table 2: Some rules added by adjunct factorization

X	$\rightarrow$	⟨ those workers have shown , hebben de medewerkers bewezen ⟩
X	$\rightarrow$	⟨ those $X^{[1]}$ have shown , hebben de $X^{[1]}$ bewezen ⟩
X	$\rightarrow$	⟨ those workers have $X^{[1]}$, hebben de medewerkers $X^{[1]}$ ⟩
X	$\rightarrow$	⟨ $X^{[1]}$ have $X^{[2]}$, hebben $X^{[1]}$ $X^{[2]}$ ⟩

The combinations of adjuncts that can be excised from a phrase grow exponentially with the number of adjuncts in the phrase. Even if this number remains small in general, adjunct factorization is applied to all phrases, in an extraction space that is already increased by extending extraction-phrase spans. Besides, the number of adjuncts in a phrase may also be high occasionally, especially since we regard enumeration tails as adjuncts. This concern motivates the hierarchical nesting of enumerated elements presented in section 2.

We contain grammar size increase by excising one adjunct at a time in adjunct-group phrases, and one adjunct group (or stand-alone adjunct) at a time in other phrases.

The adjunct factorization we propose for Hiero is incomplete as it does not fully extract adjuncts from phrase pairs. Compared to STAG, our grammar extracts 'derived' rules with generalized adjunction patterns, rather than separating 'auxiliary' from 'initial' rules. Consequently, our grammar increases in size rather than becoming more compact.

4 Experiments

4.1 Data

We performed experiments on three language pairs: English-Chinese, English-Dutch and English-French. For all experiments, word alignments were obtained using GIZA++ with 'grow-diag-final-and' symmetrization (Och and Ney, 2003). The English side of the data were parsed using the Turbo parser, and converted to adjunct parses following the criteria of section 2. We used a 4-gram language model, trained with KenLM (Heafield et al., 2013).

The English-Chinese data were taken from the MultiUN corpus (Eisele and Chen, 2010), limited to sentences of up to 40 tokens. We first extracted an in-domain development and test set by randomly drawing 4000 sentences without replacement from the corpus (after having removed English-side duplicates), and splitting the resulting set in two. Word alignments were trained on the rest of the corpus (ca. 5.6M sentence pairs). The language model was trained on the Xinhua section of the Chinese Gigaword corpus (LDC2003T09).

The English-Dutch data were taken from the Europarl corpus (v7). We extracted a development and test set of 2000 sentence pairs each following the same method as for the English-Chinese data. The language model was trained on the target side of the training corpus.

The English-French data were taken from the Europarl corpus (v7), limited to sentences of up to 40 tokens. We used the Europarl 2006 development and test sets, and trained the language model on the target side of the corpus.

For English-Chinese, we used training sets of two different sizes. Table 3 summarizes the sizes and average sentence length of the different data sets.

Table 3: Data-set sizes

		train		dev	test
fr	sentences	500k		2k	2k
	avg. tokens	20.6		29.0	29.7
nl	sentences	500k		2k	2k
	avg. tokens	27.4		27.6	27.1
zh	sentences	500k	2M	2k	2k
	avg. tokens	22.5	22.5	22.7	22.6

4.2 Tuning and Decoding

All models use an extended set of dense features (not counting adjunction features), following Maillette de Buy Wenniger and Sima'an (2013). Feature weights are tuned with MIRA (Cherry and Foster, 2012), for 20 iterations.

Decoding is performed with Joshua (Li et al., 2009), with a relaxation of the decoding span to 100 tokens. This allows hierarchical rules to span an entire sentence in the case of the extended models.

4.3 Adjunction-based-model results

Results for English-Chinese, with a small training set

Table 4 presents test results on the smaller English-Chinese training set (500k sentence pairs). These tests compare the adjunction-based models, with and without labelling or features, to a Hiero baseline. We also tested the effect of relaxing the decoding span on Hiero. We use the following identifiers for the models: `H-100` is a Hiero model with a relaxed decoding span, `adj` uses adjunction-based constraints, but no labels or adjunction features; `adj-F` also uses the *long-distance* and *adjunct-crossing* features; `adj-L` uses labels (including adjunct-sequence labels); `adj-FL` uses both features and labels; `adj-L2F` replaces the adjunct-sequence labels by their corresponding feature.

Table 4: Experimental results for English-Chinese; training set size=500k[a]

	Hiero	H-100	adj	adj-F	adj-L	adj-FL	adj-L2F
BLEU	21.8	21.7	21.5*	22.0	22.1*	22.3*	22.3*
BEER	11.2	11.2	11.1	11.3	11.4*	11.4*	11.4*
TER	63.8	64.4*	64.1*	64.1*	64.3*	63.9	64.3*
LENGTH	99.8	100.1*	98.1*	99.5*	100.0*	99.7	99.8
LR-KB1[b]	0.265	0.262	0.258	0.260	0.261	0.263	0.261

[a] We mark significance levels of $p = 0.05$; each model was tuned and decoded three times.
[b] The LR-KB1 scores were computed giving equal weight to BLEU-1 and Kendall's tau ($\alpha = 0.5$)

While extending extraction spans with the `adj` model decreases performance, both labelling and the base adjunction features allow to guide decoding in the adjunct-driven models, and outperform Hiero, both in terms of BLEU and BEER (Stanojević and Sima'an, 2014). The highest improvements are obtained for the models employing both labelling and features, with little or no difference between the full-label model `adj-FL` and the label-to-feature model `adj-L2F`. The lack of improvement in LR score (Birch and Osborne, 2011) suggest that the adjunct-driven models improve lexical selection rather than reordering.

Effect of training set size

Table 5 presents results for the larger English-Chinese data set (2M training sentence pairs). With a larger data set, relaxing the decoding span for Hiero (`H-100`) is beneficial for English-Chinese–locally learned rules are useful when applied to larger spans. As before, extending extraction spans alone decreases performance, but labels and features allow to guide the model and improve performance; the `adj-L2F` model outperforms Hiero by 0.6 BLEU point.

Table 5: Experimental results for English-Chinese; training set size=2M

	Hiero	H-100	adj	adj-L2F
BLEU	23.2	23.5*	23.0	23.8*
BEER	12.5	12.6	12.5	12.8
TER	61.9	62.0	61.4*	62.1
LENGTH	98.9	98.7	96.9*	99.1
LR-KB1	0.272	0.268	0.268	0.270

[a] Results are based on two tuning runs

Tests on other language pairs

Table 6 presents results for English-French and English-Dutch for training sets of 500k sentence pairs. We find that the adjunction-driven model performs similarly to Hiero for both these language pairs.

Table 6: Experimental results for English-Dutch and English-French; training size=500k

	en-nl				en-fr			
	Hiero	H-100	adj	adj-L2F	Hiero	H-100	adj	adj-L2F
BLEU	27.5	27.5	27.5	27.4	32.9	32.8	33.0	32.7
BEER	16.4	16.3	16.4	16.3	23.6	23.6	23.6	23.5
TER	59.5	59.6	59.5	59.6	53.9	54.3	53.9	54.1
LENGTH	99.9	100.3	99.8	99.7	99.1	99.3	99.3	99.3
LR-KB1	0.307	0.307	0.306	0.305	0.390	0.388	0.390	0.389

[a] Results are based on a single tuning round

Inspection of output translations shows several cases of improved lexical selection for French. For instance, the `adj-L2F` model is able to capture the dependency between 'enthusiasm' and 'wane' in the first example in Table 7, and to translate both words appropriately. One also can find examples of improved reordering, as in the second example in the table. While both Hiero and the `adj-L2F` model wrongly reorder the translations of 'geopolitical' and 'geographical', making them appear as dependents of 'outpost' and 'population' respectively, the `adj-L2F` model is able, unlike Hiero, to preserve the dependency between 'outpost' and 'of europe'.

Table 7: Example translations

Improved lexical selection	
src	the problem is that , if you set a date , there is a danger that the enthusiasm for reform in these countries will wane .
Hiero	le problème est que , si vous wane fixer une date , il y a un risque que l' enthousiasme de réforme dans ces pays .
adj-L2F	le problème est que , si vous fixer une date , il y a un risque que l' enthousiasme de réforme dans ces pays diminue .
Limited reordering improvement	
src	because of its geopolitical position as the last outpost of europe , at the crossroads with the middle east and north africa , the importance of malta goes far beyond its geographical size and its small population.
Hiero	en raison de sa position en tant que dernier retranchement géopolitique , au carrefour avec le moyen-orient et l' afrique du nord , l' importance de malte va bien au-delà de sa taille et sa petite population géographique de l' europe .
adj-L2F	en raison de sa position en tant que dernier retranchement géopolitique de l' europe , à la croisée des chemins avec le moyen-orient et l' afrique du nord , l' importance de malte va bien au-delà de sa taille et sa petite population géographique .

Adjunct factorization model

Table 8 presents preliminary results for the adjunct factorization model of section 3.2 (`adj-Opt`). While this model does not use adjunction or features, the gap in performance with regard to Hiero appears bigger than for the `adj` model.

5 Discussion

We have presented an adjunction-based hierarchical phrase-based model, that extends Hiero in two ways: by letting adjuncts guide the extraction of larger phrase pairs, and by marking adjuncts through labelling.

Our model outperforms Hiero for English-Chinese on training sets of moderate size (500k and 2M sentence pairs), by 0.5 and 0.6 BLEU points respectively. The improvement is brought by the combination of extraction features with a minimal adjunct/non-adjunct source labelling scheme. This is a very positive result, that shows that the adjunct/argument distinction can be useful for machine translation, even

Table 8: Experimental results for the adjunct-optionality model, for English-Chinese

	training=500k				training=2M			
	BLEU	BEER	TER	LEN	BLEU	BEER	TER	LEN
Hiero	21.7	11.1	64.6	100.0	23.4	12.6	62.0	98.8
adj-Opt	21.0**	10.9	64.1*	97.9**	22.8**	12.3	61.8	97.5**

[a] Results are based on a single tuning round

though our means to identify adjuncts are coarse (in the example of Figure 1 for instance, "to the solar power industry" is argueably an argument of "made the switch", and not an adjunct). Beside we assumed here that source adjuncts project into target adjuncts. This is an optimistic assumption (Hwa et al., 2002; Arnoult and Sima'an, 2014), and we are bound to extract many erroneous rules. The adjunct-driven model is however able to guide the model sufficiently well to ward off these rules for English-Chinese. Refining the labels and features is likely to further enhance the model.

While our feature set may be improved, we face the difficulty that the current features are informative of the extraction of a rule, and we accordingly store their values along with the rules in the grammar. This increases the size occupied by the grammar in memory, making it harder to extract grammars for larger training sets.

We found that the adjunct-driven model provides no improvement over Hiero for English-Dutch and English-French. We believe that the improvement for English-Chinese is related to the extent of reordering in this language pair: while system scores suggest a mostly lexical improvement, reordering in English-Chinese may favor the application of hierarchical rules (rather than glue rules), and benefit more from the linguistic constraint brought by the adjunct-driven model.

Additionally, we have presented another extension, that leverages adjunct optionality to extract rules by excising adjuncts and their projections, following what Arnoult and Sima'an (2012) had done for a phrase-based model. The resulting model underperforms Hiero for English-Chinese, and while an adapted feature and label set may improve results, selecting which adjuncts to excise appears necessary.

6 Conclusion

We have presented an adjunct-driven extension to Hiero: the model uses source-side adjuncts to extract larger phrases and to label rules. The model is able to improve over Hiero for English-Chinese with minimal labelling and a few features. This improvement appears to be mostly lexical: the model captures long-distance dependencies better, but not long-distance reorderings. We found no improvement for English-Dutch and English-French. The lesser extent of reordering in these language pairs may limit the application of rules involving adjuncts; further constraining the model may then be beneficial for these language pairs too.

We have also presented a second extension, that factors adjunction to derive rules with simpler adjunction patterns. This extension leads to a decrease in performance compared to Hiero: while an adapted feature and label set may help this model, constraints on which adjuncts to excise are likely to be necessary as well.

Acknowledgments

This research is part of the project "Statistical Translation of Novel Constructions", which is supported by NWO VC EW grant 612.001.122 from the Netherlands Organisation for Scientific Research (NWO).

References

Hala Almaghout, Jie Jiang, and Andy Way. 2011. CCG contextual labels in hierarchical phrase-based SMT. In *Proceedings of the 15th conference of the European Association for Machine Translation*, pages 281–288.

Sophie Arnoult and Khalil Sima'an. 2012. Adjunct Alignment in Translation Data with an Application to Phrase-Based Statistical Machine Translation. In *Proceedings of the 16th Annual Conference of the European Association for Machine Translation*, pages 287–294.

Sophie Arnoult and Khalil Sima'an. 2014. How Synchronous are Adjuncts in Translation Data? In *Proceedings of SSST-8, Eighth Workshop on Syntax, Semantics and Structure in Statistical Translation*, pages 157–165, Doha, Qatar.

Alexandra Birch and Miles Osborne. 2011. Reordering Metrics for MT. In *Proceedings of the Association for Computational Linguistics*, Portland, Oregon, USA.

Colin Cherry and George Foster. 2012. Batch Tuning Strategies for Statistical Machine Translation. In *Proceedings of the 2012 Conference of the North American Chapter of the Association for Computational Linguistics: Human Language Technologies*, pages 427–436, Montréal, Canada.

David Chiang. 2000. Statistical Parsing with an Automatically-Extracted Tree Adjoining Grammar. In *Proceedings of the 38th Annual Meeting of the Association for Computational Linguistics*, pages 456–463.

David Chiang. 2005. A Hierarchical Phrase-Based Model for Statistical Machine Translation. In *Proceedings of the 43rd Annual Meeting of the Association for Computational Linguistics*, pages 263–270.

Steve DeNeefe and Kevin Knight. 2009. Synchronous Tree Adjoining Machine Translation. In *Proceedings of the 2009 Conference on Empirical Methods in Natural Language Processing*, pages 727–736.

Andreas Eisele and Yu Chen. 2010. MultiUN: A Multilingual Corpus from United Nation Documents. In *Proceedings of the Seventh conference on International Language Resources and Evaluation (LREC'10)*, Valletta, Malta.

Kenneth Heafield, Ivan Pouzyrevsky, Jonathan H. Clark, and Philipp Koehn. 2013. Scalable modified Kneser-Ney language model estimation. In *Proceedings of the 51st Annual Meeting of the Association for Computational Linguistics*, pages 690–696, Sofia, Bulgaria.

Matthias Huck, Stephan Peitz, Markus Freitag, and Hermann Ney. 2012. Discriminative Reordering Extensions for Hierarchical Phrase-Based Machine Translation. In *16th Annual Conference of the European Association for Machine Translation*, pages 313–320, Trento, Italy.

Rebecca Hwa, Philip Resnik, Amy Weinberg, and Okan Kolak. 2002. Evaluating Translational Correspondence Using Annotation Projection. In *Proceedings of the 40th Annual Meeting on Association for Computational Linguistics*, ACL '02, pages 392–399.

Aravind K. Joshi and Yves Schabes. 1997. Tree-Adjoining Grammars. In G. Rosenberg and A. Salomaa, editors, *Handbook of Formal Languages*. Springer-Verlag, New York, NY.

Aravind K. Joshi, Leon S. Levy, and Masako Takahashi. 1975. Tree Adjunct Grammars. *Journal of Computer and System Sciences*, 10(1):136–163.

Philipp Koehn, Franz Josef Och, and Daniel Marcu. 2003. Statistical Phrase-Based Translation. In *Proceedings of HLT/NAACL*, pages 127–133.

Anthony Kroch and Aravind Joshi. 1985. The Linguistic Relevance of Tree Adjoining Grammars. Technical Report MC CIS 85 18, Department of Computer and Information Science, University of Pennsylvania.

Zhifei Li, Chris Callison-Burch, Chris Dyer, Sanjeev Khudanpur, Lane Schwartz, Wren Thornton, Jonathan Weese, and Omar Zaidan. 2009. Joshua: An open source toolkit for parsing-based machine translation. In *Proceedings of the Fourth Workshop on Statistical Machine Translation*, pages 135–139, Athens, Greece.

Junhui Li, Zhaopeng Tu, Guodong Zhou, and Josef van Genabith. 2012. Using Syntactic Head Information in Hierarchical Phrase-Based Translation. In *Proceedings of the 7th Workshop on Statistical Machine Translation*, pages 232–242.

Junhui Li, Philip Resnik, and Hal Daumé III. 2013. Modeling Syntactic and Semantic Structures in Hierarchical Phrase-based Translation. In *Proceedings of the 2013 Conference of the North American Chapter of the Association for Computational Linguistics: Human Language Technologies*, pages 540–549, Atlanta, Georgia.

Gideon Maillette de Buy Wenniger and Khalil Sima'an. 2013. Hierarchical Alignment Decomposition Labels for Hiero Grammar Rules. In *Proceedings of the Seventh Workshop on Syntax, Semantics and Structure in Statistical Translation*, pages 19–28, Atlanta, Georgia.

Markos Mylonakis and Khalil Sima'an. 2011. Learning Hierarchical Translation Structure with Linguistic Annotation. In *Proceedings of the 49th Annual Meeting of the Association for Computational Linguistics*, pages 642–652.

Franz Josef Och and Hermann Ney. 2003. A Systematic Comparison of Various Statistical Alignment Models. *Computational Linguistics*, 29:19–51.

Stuart Shieber and Yves Schabes. 1990. Synchronous Tree-Adjoining Grammars. In *Handbook of Formal Languages*, pages 69–123. Springer.

Stuart M. Shieber. 2007. Probabilistic Synchronous Tree-Adjoining Grammars for Machine Translation: The Argument from Bilingual Dictionaries. In *Proceedings of the Workshop on Syntax and Structure in Statistical Translation*, Rochester, New York.

Miloš Stanojević and Khalil Sima'an. 2014. Evaluating Word Order Recursively over Permutation-Forests. In *Proceedings of SSST-8, Eighth Workshop on Syntax, Semantics and Structure in Statistical Translation*, pages 138–147, Doha, Qatar.

Andreas Zollmann and Ashish Venugopal. 2006. Syntax Augmented Machine Translation via Chart Parsing. In *Proceedings of NAACL 2006 - Workshop on statistical machine translation*, pages 138–141.

A Hybrid Approach for Deep Machine Translation

Kiril Simov
Linguistic Modelling Department
IICT-BAS
Bulgaria
kivs@bultreebank.org

Petya Osenova
Linguistic Modelling Department
IICT-BAS
Bulgaria
petya@bultreebank.org

Abstract

This paper presents a Hybrid Approach to Deep Machine Translation in the language direction from English to Bulgarian. The set-up uses pre- and post-processing modules as well as two-level transfer. The language resources that have been incorporated are: WordNets for both languages; a valency lexicon for Bulgarian; aligned parallel corpora. The architecture comprises a predominantly statistical component (factor-based SMT in Moses) with some focused rule-based elements. The experiments show promising results and room for further improvements within the MT architecture.

1 Introduction

The paper presents a hybrid approach for Deep Semantic Machine Translation. For that purpose, however, the linguistic phenomena that constitute deep semantics have to be defined. A list of such phenomena have been considered in (Hajič, 2011) and (Bos, 2013), among others. They include but are not limited to the following ones: Semantic Roles (words vs. predicates, Lexical Semantics (Word Sense Disambiguation (WSD)), Multiword Expressions (MWE), Logical Form (LF), Metonymy, Named Entities (NE), Co-reference (pronominal, bridging anaphora), Verb Phrase Ellipsis, Collective/Distributive NPs, Scope (Negation, Quantifiers), Presuppositions, Tense and Aspect, Illocution Force, Textual Entailment, Discourse Structure/ Rhetorical Relations, neo-Davidsonian Events, Background Knowledge, Information Structure etc. All the mentioned phenomena represent various levels of granularity and different linguistic dimensions.

In our deep Machine Translation (MT) system we decided to exploit the following components in the transfer phase: Lexical Semantics (WSD), MultiWord Expression (MWE), Named Entities (NE) and Logical Form (LF). For the incorporation of Lexical Semantics through the exploitation of WordNet and Valency dictionary the knowledge-based approach to WSD has been accepted. Concerning the LF, we rely on Minimal Recursion Semantics (MRS) in its two variants - the full one (MRS) and the more underspecified one (Robust MRS (RMRS)). The MWE and NE are parts of the lexicons. We should note that there are also other appropriate LF frameworks that are briefly mentioned below.

One of the MRS-related semantic formalisms is the Abstract Meaning Representation (AMR[1]), which aims at achieving whole-sentence deep semantics instead of addressing various isolated holders of semantic information (such as, NER, coreferences, temporal anchors, etc.). AMR also builds on the available syntactic trees, thus contributing to the efforts on sembanking. It is English-dependent and it makes an extensive use of PropBank framesets (Kingsbury and Palmer, 2002) and (Palmer et al., 2005). Its concepts are either English words or special keywords. AMR uses approximately 100 relations. They include: frame arguments, general semantic relations, relations for quantities and date-entities, etc.

The Groningen Meaning Bank (GMB) integrates various phenomena in one formalism. It has a linguistically motivated, theoretically solid (CCG[2]/DRT[3]) background.

[1]http://www.isi.edu/natural-language/amr/a.pdf

[2]Combinatory Categorical Grammar

[3]Discourse Representation Theory

Proceedings of the 2nd Deep Machine Translation Workshop (DMTW 2016), pages 21–28,
Lisbon, Portugal, 21 October 2016.

In this paper the NLP strategies are presented for Hybrid Deep Machine Translation in the direction from English-to-Bulgarian. Under Hybrid MT we understand the usage of the automatic Moses system together with a rule-based component at the transfer phase.

The paper is structured as follows:in section 2 the components of the hybrid MT architecture is presented. Section 3 discusses the deep semantic processing. Section 4 reports on the current experiments and results. Section 5 concludes the paper.

2 A Hybrid MT Architecture

Our Hybrid MT Architecture (see Fig. 1) includes the following components: NLP preprocessing of the source language (in this case English)(statistical approach); projection of the annotations on the tokens in the text (statistical); first-level transfer where the source tokens are substituted as much as possible with their translations in the target language and an intermediate language is created (rule-based and statistical); second-level transfer where the translations are based on the lemma (statistical); generation is performed (statistical) and post-processing is applied (rule-based).

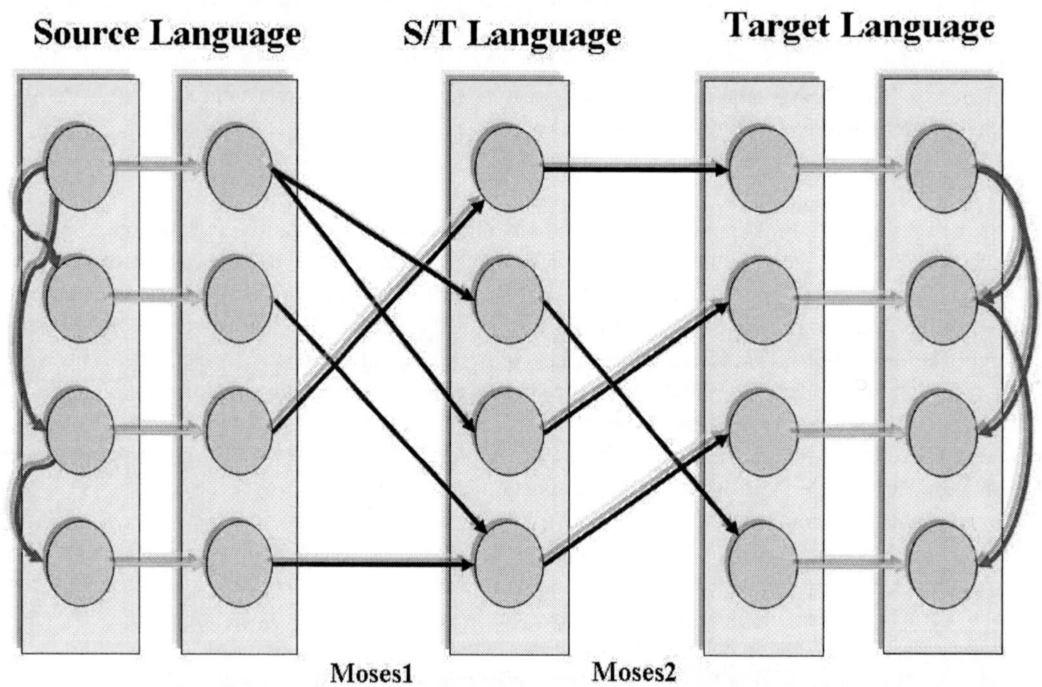

Figure 1: A Hybrid Architecture for Transferring of Linguistic Information from the Source to the Target Language. The linguistic analyses for the source language are projected to a tokinized source text; then Moses models are applied for producing a target language translation. The translation alignment is used for transferring the information to the corresponding tokens in the target language and is used for post processing.

The NLP preprocessing uses the Core NLP package tool for English. The result from the linguistic processing is stored on token level in the source text. The translation steps are performed by a pipeline of two Moses models (Moses1 and Moses2 in the Fig. 1). The first Moses model is phrase based trained on Europarl, Setimes, LibreOffice parallel corpora. The result is used to form intermediate text (Source/Target Language (S/T) text). The construction of S/L text is based on Word Sense Disambiguation similar to approach described in (Simov et al., 2016): it substitutes the words based on the inferred WordNet synsets (if available) and the substitution rules from English to Bulgarian. They take the most frequent lemma in the Bulgarian synset (calculated against a corpus of 70 million words) doctor#1, doc#1, physician#1, MD#2, Dr.#2, medico#2 = doktor#1, lekar#1, d-r#1. Additionally, some words in the source language are transferred to the target language lemmas on the basis of the results from Moses model one (Moses1). The second-level transfer is achieved through training Moses (Moses2 in the figure) on the factored, partially translated corpus from the first level transfer. It replaces the word-form with a representative lemma from the WordNet synset in the target language: napredak|progress|nn.

The alignment between the source text and the target text created during the translation with Moses system is used for transferring of linguistic information from the source linguistic analysis to the target translation. Here is an example of such an alignment of the sentence "Place them in the midst of a pile of dirty, wet soccer kit." and its translation into Bulgarian[4]:

```
(place them in) = (postavyaneto im v)
(the midst of) = (razgar na)
(a pile of) = (kup)
(dirty) = (izmyrsyavam)
(,) = (,)
(soccer) = (futbolni)
(kit) = (komplekt)
(.) = (.)
```

The transferred information is then used in the postprocessing phase. It should be noted that the alignment between Source Language to S/T Language and from S/T Language to Target is not one-to-one. It maps sequences from the source language to sequences in the target language and the transfer of the linguistic information from the analysis of the source language to the target is not straightforward. Thus, we use heuristic rules. In practice, about 80% of the correspondences are between one-to-one or two-to-two tokens. This facilitates the transfer of the information. But the transferred information is only partial. For the definition of the rules we exploit also language resources and tools for the target language.

In the experiments we use four sets of parallel data (QTLeap corpus: Batch1 to Batch4) and several versions of the translation systems (Baseline, Pilot1, Pilot2 and Pilot3). In this hybrid architecture we use the baseline as Moses1 model and Pilot2 with an extended WordNet as Moses2 one. The current results from for EN-to-BG on Batch4 (answers part) of the QTLeap corpus are as follows: Baseline: 19.91 BLEU (no factors); Pilot2: 20.24 BLEU.

The generation phase relies completely on the Moses system. Then, in the post processing step, a rule-based system is applied, based on lingusitically-enhanced information. It includes various types of rules: morphological, syntactic and semantic. An example of a syntactic rule is the transformation of the English NN compounds into the appropriate syntactic structures in Bulgarian. The direct transfer is rare, since the NN compounds are not so frequent in Bulgarian. They would hold for phrases like "business meeting", for example. An interesting fact in this type is the transposition of N1 and N2 from English to Bulgarian in the N2 N1 variant. It happens when N1 is a named entity. For example, "Rila mountain" is translated as "planina Rila" (mountain Rila). The more frequent types are: adjective noun (AN) and noun with a prepositional phrase (NpN).

3 Deep Semantic Processing

In order to fulfil the demands of MT, deep semantic processing must have at its disposal a considerable amount of *semantic language resources* such as syntax/semantic treebanks (DeepBank, Prague Dependency Treebank, PropBank, Groningen Meaning Bank, etc.), semantic lexicons (WordNet, Ontology-based Lexicons, Valency Lexicons, etc.), and background knowledge (ontologies, linked open data, etc.), *which complement the semantic content of the text in considerable depth and scope*. This definition allows for many approaches to semantic processing to be considered as deep semantic processing.

Deep semantic processing might be and in most cases is still language dependent to a great extent. For instance, the predicates involved in the analyses could be based on the lemmas of the word forms in the

[4]Please note that the examples from Bulgarian are presented in their transliterated equivalents.

sentences. The addition of background knowledge provides some language independent elements in the semantic content of the text and we hope that this ensures a better semantic transfer.

In this section we present the main parameters behind the Minimal Recursion Semantics (MRS) as an example of underspecified semantic formalisms. MRS underspecifies scope ambiguities for quantifiers and other scope-bearing elements. The selection of MRS is motivated by several facts: (1) it has already been implemented as part of HPSG grammars for several project languages: English (Copestake and Flickinger, 2000), German (Crysmann, 2007), Spanish (Marimon et al., 2007), Portuguese (Branco and Costa, 2008), (Costa and Branco, 2010) and Bulgarian (Osenova, 2010); (2) it is already used as a basis for semantic transfer in MT systems for several language pairs — (Bond et al., 2005) and (Oepen et al., 2004); (3) it allows the construction of semantic representation over shallow analyses or dependency syntactic structures — (Copestake, 20042006), (Copestake, 2007); (4) there exist corpora annotated with MRS structures, including some parallel ones — (Flickinger et al., 2012b) and (Flickinger et al., 2012a).

At the same time, it should be noted that the existence of precise and robust linguistic grammars for various languages requires time-and labour-consuming work, in spite of the attempts of the community to provide various start-up kits for better enhancement of new languages. Thus, at the moment the ERG grammar for English is well developed and ready for real applications. Close to it are the grammars for Japanese, Spanish, Norwegian, etc., but in general the current available grammars for many other languages seem to be under-developed and toy-suited. Another issue is that it is challenging to produce full MRSes from dependency parses. Thus, the concept of RMRS is more suitable for real MT applications, in which the production of the logical forms is partial.

3.1 Minimal Recursion Semantics Representation

3.1.1 MRS Definition

MRS is introduced as an underspecified semantic formalism (Copestake et al., 2005). It is used to support semantic analyses in the HPSG English Resource Grammar — (Copestake and Flickinger, 2000), but also in other grammar formalisms like LFG. The main idea is the formalism to rule out spurious analyses resulting from the representation of logical operators and the scope of quantifiers. Spurious analyses of logical form over an utterance could be result from different NLP analyses which produce equivalent logical but syntactically different expressions, like the following two formulas: $\lambda x[\text{fierce}(x) \wedge (\text{black}(x) \wedge \text{cat}(x))]$ and $\lambda x[\text{cat}(x) \wedge (\text{black}(x) \wedge \text{fierce}(x))]$. In MRS such spurious analyses are excluded by the flat representation of the body in the formulas. The determination of the scope of quantifiers in a sentence very often requires information which is not available during the sentence processing. Thus, MRS provides a compact representation which allows further specialization of the quantifiers scope when the necessary information becomes available.

Here we will present only basic definitions from (Copestake et al., 2005). For more details the cited publication should be consulted. An MRS structure is a tuple $< GT, R, C >$, where GT is the top handle, R is a bag of EPs (elementary predicates) and C is a bag of handle constraints, such that there is no handle h that outscopes GT. Each elementary predication contains exactly four components: (1) a handle which is the label of the EP; (2) a relation; (3) a list of zero or more ordinary variable arguments of the relation; and (4) a list of zero or more handles corresponding to scopal arguments of the relation (i.e., holes). Each scopal argument could be assigned to a handle. In this way the elementary predicates with this handle become arguments of other elementary predicates. For example, a quantifier requires such kind of arguments as a body or restriction of the quantifier. Thus handles are used to represent different readings of the same set of elementary predicates via different assignments from handles to the corresponding arguments — see the example below, taken from the cited paper. The handle constraints have the following form: $h_i = h_j$ which states that h_i outscopes h_j. Here is an example of a complex MRS structure for the sentence "Every dog chases some white cat."

$$< h_0, \{h_1 : every(x, h_2, h_3), h_2 : dog(x), h_4 : chase(x, y), h_5 : some(y, h_6, h_7),$$

$$h_6 : white(y), h_6 : cat(y)\}, \{\} >$$

The top handle is h_0. The two quantifiers are represented as relations $every(x, y, z)$ and $some(x, y, z)$ where x is the bound variable, y and z are handles determining the restriction and the body of the quantifier. The conjunction of two or more relations is represented by sharing the same handle (h_6 above). The outscope relation is defined as a transitive closure of the immediate outscope relation between two elementary predications — EP immediately outscopes EP' iff one of the scopal arguments of EP is the label of EP'. In this example the set of handle constraints is empty, which means that the representation is underspecified with respect to the scope of both quantifiers. The representation of the MRS structure via bags of elementary predicates and handle constraints allows an easy definition of compositional rules via union of bags and variable substitution. This feature of the MRS provides an easy mechanism for implementation of MRS processors in combination with a syntactic parsing.

3.1.2 RMRS Definition

Robust Minimal Recursion Semantics (RMRS) is introduced as a modification of MRS which captures the semantics resulting from a shallow analysis — see (Copestake, 20042006) and (Copestake, 2007). The main motivations for this development are the facts that currently no single system can do everything: both deep and shallow processing have inherent strengths and weaknesses; on the other hand, the domain-dependent and domain-independent processing must be linked. The ideal level on which this linking can take place is semantics. Therefore, (Copestake, 20042006) and (Copestake, 2007) propose a semantic representation which allows to build a comparable semantic representation for both deep and shallow processing. The justification behind RMRS is to add more underspecification to MRS. This is done by e.g. the separation of arguments from the predicates. Thus each predicate is represented via its name (constructed on the basis of the lemma of the word form in the text) and its main argument which depends on the part of speech - *referential index* for nouns and some pronouns or *event index* in other cases. In this way it is possible that the predicates and their arguments are added to the structure separately from each other. Here we present a formal definition of RMRS as defined in (Jakob et al., 2010). An RMRS structure is a quadruple

$$< hook, EPbag, argumentset, handleconstraints >$$

where a hook consists of three elements $l : a : i$, l is a label, a is an anchor and i is an index. Each elementary predication is additionally marked with an anchor[5] — $l : a : r(i)$, where l is a label, a is an anchor and $r(i)$ is a relation with one argument of appropriate kind — referential index or event index. The argument set contains argument statements of the following kind $a : ARG(x)$, where a is anchor which determines for which relation the argument is defined, ARG is the name of the argument, and x is an index or a hole variable or handle (h) for scopal predicates. The handle constraints are of the form $h =_q l$, where h is a handle, l is a label and $=_q$ is the relation expressing the constraint similarly to MRS. $=_q$ sometimes is written as qeq.

Both representations MRS and RMRS could be transferred to each other under certain conditions. For MRS-to-RMRS it will be necessary to have access to the word forms in the text from which the corresponding predicates were inferred. For RMRS-to-MRS it will be necessary to unify the number of arguments of predicates via some kind of a lexicon. The separation of the predicates from their arguments facilitates the construction of RMRS structures over shallow analyses. Shallow processors usually do not have access to a lexicon. Thus they cannot predict the amount of the arguments that have the corresponding predicate. The forming of the relation names follows such conventions that provide possibilities to construct a correct semantic representation only on the base of information provided by a POS tagger, for example.

3.2 MRS Processing

As it was mentioned above, the RMRS analyses generate over partial and shallow analyses. The idea is to extract as much as possible semantic information from a partial or shallow processed text. In the worst

[5]The anchors determine the tokens which generate the corresponding elementary predicates and related arguments. This information facilitates the transfer of information from the source text to target one.

case — from POS tagged text. (Copestake, 2007) demonstrates how RMRS structures can be constructed over the output of a robust statistical parser RASP, which does not have access to subcategorisation information (Briscoe and Carroll, 2002).

The input for the RMRS structures module is based on the following linguistic annotation — the lemma ($Lemma$) for the given wordform; the morphosyntactic tag ($MSTag$) of the wordform, and the dependent relations (Rel) in the dependency tree. In cases of quantifiers we have access to the lexicon used in the Bulgarian HPSG grammar. The algorithm for producing of RMRS from a dependency parse is implemented via two types of rules:

$$< Lemma, MSTag > \to EP - RMRS$$

The rules of this type produce an RMRS structure representing an elementary predicate.

$$< DRMRS, Rel, HRMRS > HRMRS'$$

The rules of this type unite the RMRS constructed for a dependent node ($DRMRS$) into the current RMRS for a head node ($HRMRS$). The union ($HRMRS'$) is determined by the dependency relation (Rel) between the two nodes.

First, we start with assigning EPs for each lemma in the dependency tree. These EPs are similar to node EPs of (Jakob et al., 2010). Each EP for a given lemma consists of a predicate generated on the basis of the lemma string. Additionally, the morphosyntactic features of the wordform are presented. On the basis of the part-of-speech tag the type of ARG0 is determined — referential index or event index. After this initial step the basic RMRS structure for each lemma in the sentence is compiled. Then these structures are incorporated in each other in bottom-up manner. Here are examples of two RMRS structures constructed in this way. They are in Bulgarian: (1) an RMRS for the verb *'cheta'* (to read):

$< l1 : a1 : e1, \{l1 : a1 :\text{cheta\_}v\_rel(e1)\}, \{a1 : ARG1(x1)\}, \{\} >$

In this example we also include information for the unexpressed subject (ARG1) which is always incorporated in the verb form. The RMRS structure for a sentence with an explicit subject and an explicit direct object follows. The sentence is *momche mu chete kniga* [Boy him-dative reads book], 'A boy reads a book to him')[6]:

$< l2 : a3 : e1,$
$\{l1 : a1 :\text{momche\_}n\_rel(x1), l2 : a3 :\text{chete\_}v\_rel(e1), l3 : a4 :\text{kniga\_}n\_rel(x2)\},$
$\{a3 : ARG1(x1), a3 : ARG2(x2), a3 : ARG3(x3)\},$
$\{\} >$

The construction of RMRS for sentences, based on shallow processing, suffers from the pipeline processing effect — error accumulation. Errors in earlier processing stages cause suboptimal performance during the next steps.

3.3 MRS for Deep Semantic Transfer in MT

Minimal Recursion Semantics was originally developed for the purposes of Machine Translation. The main idea was that an underspecified semantic representation is appropriate for machine translation because it provides an abstract level to semantic transfer, but at the same time it postpones the difficult decisions. These difficulties are assumed to be less important in the area of machine translation. MRS was applied in the past in two ways to support machine translation: (1) rule-based semantic transfer, and (2) factor-based statistical machine translation. The rules-based semantic transfer uses transfer rules working on the MRS representation of the source language MRS structures and constructing the target language MRS structure. Thus, the transfer rules in this framework are rewriting rules over MRS (Minimal Recursion Semantics) structures. The basic format of the transfer rules is:

$[\mathcal{C} :]\mathcal{I}[!\mathcal{F}] \to \mathcal{O}$

where $\mathcal{I}$ is the *input* of the rule, $\mathcal{O}$ is the *output*. $\mathcal{C}$ determines the *context* and $\mathcal{F}$ is the *filter* of the rule. $\mathcal{C}$ selects the positive and $\mathcal{F}$ the negative context for the application of a rule. For more details on

[6]In this case the information coming from clitics is represented only in the argument set.

the transfer rules, see (Oepen, 2008). This type of rules allows an extremely flexible transfer of factual and linguistic knowledge between the source and the target languages. The rules have access to the MRS structure for the source language, but can also access the (partially) constructed target language MRS structure. Thus elements in each rule could include parts from both MRS structures. This approach requires a good deep grammar for the source language which produces complete MRS structures, then a complete set of rules for transferring of the source language MRSes to the target language MRSes and a generation grammar for the target language. As already discussed, there are no many languages equipped with such grammars and rules.

The factor-based translation model is built on top of the factored SMT model proposed by (Koehn and Hoang, 2007), as an extension of the traditional phrase-based SMT framework. Instead of using only the word form of the text, it allows the system to take a vector of factors to represent each token, both for the source and target languages. The vector of factors can be used for different levels of linguistic annotations, like lemma, part-of-speech, or other linguistic features, if they can be (somehow) represented as annotations to each token.

In our set-up we have used factored-based transfer of elementary predicates from MRSes in our earlier systems. The results were only slightly better or slightly worse than the baseline system. Thus we decided to use the hybrid system described above in order to transfer deep information from the analysis of the source language to the automatic translation in the target language where this information, together with the language resources for the target language is used for a post processing over the automatic translation.

We are still implementing rules for our hybrid approach, thus, the results we report here, are only preliminary. We have implemented transfer of the grammatical features from the source to the target language, processing of complex NE and NN compounds. The current result is 21.78 BLEU.

4 Conclusions

In this paper a hybrid architecture for deep MT was presented in the language direction from English to Bulgarian. The implementation provided some relaxation on the translation model, suggesting a two-level transfer model. The former being semantically coarse, on token level, but already using a WSD constraint; the latter being more fine-grained, on lemma level. Instead of full MRS approach, we used the RMRS variant, encoded in the factored MT model. In the post processing step some frequent errors have been corrected on morhological, syntactic and semantic levels. However, this is ongoing work. The experiments showed that this approach adds to the BLEU score results and thus is promising for further elaboration.

The actual translation approach could be different from the one presented here. Any translation system that supports alignment could be used. For example, as one of the reviewers suggested, neural network machine translation with attention could be also used. This is one direction for future work.

Acknowledgements

This research has received partial funding from the EC's FP7 under grant agreement number 610516: "QTLeap: Quality Translation by Deep Language Engineering Approaches". We are grateful to the three anonymous reviewers, whose remarks, comments, suggestions and encouragement helped us to improve the initial variant of the paper. All errors remain our own responsibility.

References

Francis Bond, Stephan Oepen, Melanie Siegel, Ann Copestake, and Dan Flickinger. 2005. Open source machine translation with DELPH-IN. In *Proceedings of the Open-Source Machine Translation Workshop at the 10th Machine Translation Summit*, pages 15 – 22.

Johan Bos. 2013. The groningen meaning bank. In *Invited Talk at Joint Symposium on Semantic Processing: Textual Inference and Structures in Corpora*.

Antonia Branco and Francisco Costa. 2008. LXGram in the Shared Task "Comparing Semantic Representations" of STEP 2008. In Johan Bos and Rodolfo Delmonte, editors, *Semantics in Text Processing. STEP 2008 Conference Proceedings*, volume 1 of *Research in Computational Semantics*, pages 299–314. College Publications.

Ted Briscoe and John Carroll. 2002. Robust accurate statistical annotation of general text. In *Proceedings of LREC-2002*, May. ACL Anthology Identifier: L02-1250.

Ann Copestake and Dan Flickinger. 2000. An open source grammar development environment and broad-coverage english grammar using hpsg. In *Proceedings of LREC-2000*.

Ann Copestake, Dan Flickinger, Carl Pollard, and Ivan Sag. 2005. Minimal recursion semantics: An introduction. *Research on Language & Computation*, 3(4):281–332.

Ann Copestake. 2004/2006. Robust minimal recursion semantics. unpublished draft.

Ann Copestake. 2007. Applying robust semantics. In *Proceedings of the 10th Conference of the Pacific Assocation for Computational Linguistics (PACLING)*, pages 1–12.

Francisco Costa and António Branco. 2010. Lxgram: A deep linguistic processing grammar for Portuguese. In *Lecture Notes in Artificial Intelligence*, volume 6001, pages 86–89. Springer, Berlin, May.

Berthold Crysmann. 2007. Local ambiguity packing and discontinuity in german. In *ACL 2007 Workshop on Deep Linguistic Processing*, pages 144–151.

Daniel Flickinger, Valia Kordoni, Yi Zhang, Antnio Branco, Kiril Simov, Petya Osenova, Catarina Carvalheiro, Francisco Costa, and Srgio Castro. 2012a. Pardeepbank: Multiple parallel deep treebanking. In *Proceedings of TLT-11*, pages 97–108. Edies Colibri, Lisbon.

Daniel Flickinger, Yi Zhang, and Valia Kordoni. 2012b. Deepbank: A dynamically annotated treebank of the wall street journal. In *Proceedings of TLT-11*, pages 85–96. Edies Colibri, Lisbon.

Jan Hajič. 2011. Machine translation research in META-NET. presentation at META-NET meeting.

Max Jakob, Markéta Lopatková, and Valia Kordoni. 2010. Mapping between dependency structures and compositional semantic representations. In *Proceedings of LREC 2010*, pages 2491–2497.

Paul Kingsbury and Martha Palmer. 2002. From treebank to propbank. In *Proceedings of LREC-2002*, pages 1989–1993.

Philipp Koehn and Hieu Hoang. 2007. Factored translation models. In *Proceedings of EMNLP*.

Montserrat Marimon, Núria Bel, Sergio Espeja, and Natalia Seghezzi. 2007. The spanish resource grammar: Pre-processing strategy and lexical acquisition. In *ACL 2007 Workshop on Deep Linguistic Processing*, pages 105–111.

Stephan Oepen, Helge Dyvik, Jan Tore Lnning, Erik Velldal, Dorothee Beermann, John Carroll, Dan Flickinger, Lars Hellan, Janne Bondi Johannessen, Paul Meurer, Torbjrn Nordgrd, and Victoria Rosn. 2004. Som kappete med trollet? Towards MRS-based Norwegian – English Machine Translation. In *Proceedings of the 10th International Conference on Theoretical and Methodological Issues in Machine Translation*.

Stephan Oepen. 2008. The Transfer Formalism. General Purpose MRS Rewriting. Technical Report LOGON Project. Technical report, University of Oslo.

Petya Osenova. 2010. *The Bulgarian Resource Grammar*. VDM.

Martha Palmer, Daniel Gildea, and Paul Kingsbury. 2005. The proposition bank: An annotated corpus of semantic roles. *Comput. Linguist.*, 31(1):71–106, March.

Kiril Simov, Petya Osenova, and Alexander Popov. 2016. Towards semantic-based hybrid machine translation between bulgarian and english. In *Proceedings of the 2nd Workshop on Semantics-Driven Machine Translation (SedMT 2016)*, pages 22–26, San Diego, California, June. Association for Computational Linguistics.

Deeper Machine Translation and Evaluation for German

Eleftherios Avramidis, Vivien Macketanz, Aljoscha Burchardt,
Jindrich Helcl and Hans Uszkoreit
German Research Center for Artificial Intelligence (DFKI)
Language Technology Lab
firstname.lastname@dfki.de

Abstract

This paper describes a hybrid Machine Translation (MT) system built for translating from English to German in the domain of technical documentation. The system is based on three different MT engines (phrase-based SMT, RBMT, neural) that are joined by a selection mechanism that uses deep linguistic features within a machine learning process. It also presents a detailed source-driven manual error analysis we have performed using a dedicated "test suite" that contains selected examples of relevant phenomena. While automatic scores show huge differences between the engines, the overall average number or errors they (do not) make is very similar for all systems. However, the detailed error breakdown shows that the systems behave very differently concerning the various phenomena.

1 Introduction

This paper describes a hybrid Machine Translation (MT) system built for translating from English to German in the domain of technical documentation. The system builds upon the general architecture described in Avramidis et al. (2016), but in the current version several components have been improved or replaced. As detailed in the previous paper, the design of the system was driven by the assumptions that a) none of today's common MT approaches, phrase-based statistical (PB-SMT) or rule-based (RBMT), is on its own capable of providing enough good translations to be useful in an outbound translation scenario without human intervention, and b) "deep" linguistic knowledge should help to improve translation quality. Instead of building a completely new system, our goal is to adjust and combine existing systems in a smart way using linguistic knowledge.

The system has been developed within the QTLeap project[1]. The goal of the project is to explore different combinations of shallow and deep processing for improving MT quality w.r.t a real use-case scenario (translating user queries and expert answers in a chat-based PC helpdesk scenario). The system presented in this paper is the final one in a series of system prototypes developed in the project. The most visible change compared to our earlier system described in (Burchardt et al., 2016a) is that we added a neural MT system for the obvious reason that this method has shown state-of-the-art performance, e.g., in the WMT-2016 translation challenge (Bojar et al., 2016). We wanted to see how this new type of SMT engine can improve our hybrid system.

In line with our general strategy to include language experts in the MT development cycle described in Burchardt et al. (2016b), we have performed a detailed source-driven error analysis using a dedicated "test suite" that contains selected examples of relevant phenomena. Especially when using MT approaches other than SMT, this makes sure that researchers striving for insights and ideas for improvement are not discouraged by using (only) automatic scores like BLEU that are by design unable to detect changes at the needed level of detail.

This paper is organised as follows: section 2 describes the component of our architecture and section 3 our evaluation efforts. Section 4 sums up and concludes the paper.

[1]QTLeap project: http://qtleap.eu/

Proceedings of the 2nd Deep Machine Translation Workshop (DMTW 2016), pages 29–38,
Lisbon, Portugal, 21 October 2016.

2 System components

Our overall hybrid architecture includes:

- A (statistical) Moses baseline system,
- the commercial transfer-based system Lucy,
- a neural MT system, and
- an informed selection mechanism ("ranker").

The architecture is illustrated in figure 1 and the different components are described below.

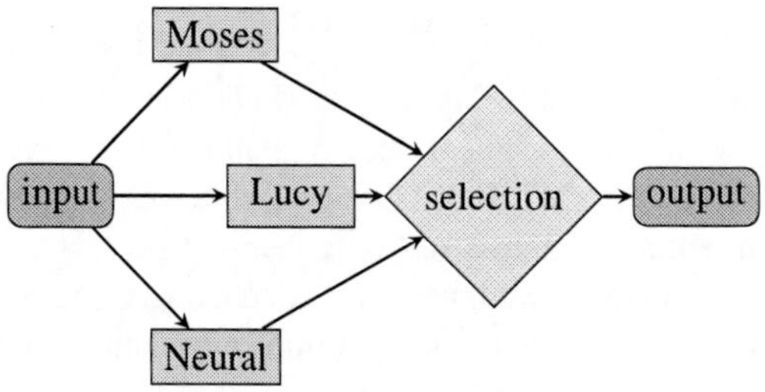

Figure 1: Architecture of the selection mechanism

2.1 Phrase-based SMT baseline

The baseline system consists of a basic phrase-based SMT model, trained with the state-of-the-art settings on both the generic and technical data. The translation table was trained on a concatenation of generic and technical data, filtering out the sentences longer than 80 words. The first batch of the QTLeap corpus[2] was used as a tuning set for MERT (Och, 2003), whereas the second batch was reserved for testing.

One language model (monolingual) of order 5 was trained on the target side from both the technical (IT-domain) and Europarl corpora, plus one language model was trained on the target-language news corpus from the years 2007 to 2013 (Callison-Burch et al., 2007). All language models were interpolated on the tuning set (Schwenk and Koehn, 2008). The size of the training data is shown in Table 1.

The text has been tokenized and truecased (Koehn et al., 2008) prior to the training and the decoding, and de-tokenized and de-truecased afterwards. A few regular expressions were added to the tokenizer, so that URLs are not tokenized before being translated. Normalization of punctuation was also included, mainly in order to fix several issues with variable typography on quotes.

The phrase-based SMT system was trained with Moses (Koehn, 2010) using EMS (Koehn, 2010), whereas the language models were trained with SRILM (Stolcke, 2002) and queried with KenLM (Heafield, 2011).

All statistical systems presented below are extensions of this system, also based on the same data and settings, unless stated otherwise.

2.2 Rule-based component

The rule-based system Lucy (Alonso and Thurmair, 2003) is also part of our experiment, due to its state-of-the-art performance in the previous years. Additionally, manual inspection on the development set has shown that it provides better handling of complex grammatical phenomena particularly when translating into German, due to the fact that it operates based on transfer rules from the source to the target syntax tree.

Additional work on RBMT focused on issues revealed through manual inspection of its performance on the QTLeap corpus (see also section 3):

[2] `http://metashare.metanet4u.eu/go2/qtleapcorpus`

corpus	entries	words
Chromium browser	6.3K	55.1K
Drupal	4.7K	57.4K
Libreoffice help	46.8K	1.1M
Libreoffice UI	35.6K	143.7K
Ubuntu Saucy	182.9K	1.6M
Europarl (mono)	2.2M	54.0M
News (mono)	89M	1.7B
Commoncrawl (parallel)	2.4M	53.6M
Europarl (parallel)	1.9M	50.1M
MultiUN (parallel)	167.6K	5.8M
News Crawl (parallel)	201.3K	5.1M

Table 1: Size of corpora used for SMT.

	BLEU	METEOR
baseline	24.90	44.38
quotes	24.00	44.29
sepMenus	25.39	45.01
sepMenus + normPunct	25.41	45.06
SMTmenus	24.06	42.83
unk	24.50	44.05
unk + sepMenus	23.68	43.30
unk + SMTmenus	25.41	44.95

Table 2: Improvements on the RBMT system measured on part of the QTLeap corpus.

- **Separate menu items**: The rule-based system was observed to be incapable of handling menu items properly, mostly when they were separated by the ">" symbol, as they often ended up as compounds. We identified the menu items by searching for consequent title-cased chunks before and after each separator. These items were translated separately from the rest of the sentence, to avoid them being bundled as compounds. The rule-based system was then forced to treat the pre-translated menu items as chunks that should not be translated.
- **Menu items by SMT**: Additionally, we used the method above to check whether menu items could be translated with the baseline phrase-based SMT system instead of Lucy.
- **Unknown words by SMT**: Since Lucy is flagging unknown words, we translated these individually with the baseline phrase-based SMT system.

Finally, we experimented with normalization of the punctuation (which was previously included in the pre-processing steps of SMT but not in RBMT), addition of quotes on the menu items and some additional automatic source pre-processing in order to remove redundant phrases such as "where it says".

We ran exhaustive search with all possible combinations of the modification above and the most indicative automatic scores are shown in table 2. Although automatic scores have in the past shown low performance when evaluating RBMT systems, our proposed modifications have a lexical impact that can be adequately measured with n-gram based metrics. Our investigation and discussion is performed on Batch 2 of the QTLeap corpus[3]. The best combination of the suggested modifications achieves an overall improvement of 0.51 points BLEU and 0.68 points METEOR over the baseline. In particular:

[3]In this paper, we will refer to Batch 1 and Batch 2 of the QTLeap corpus. This refers to the first 1000 and second 1000 sentences of the corpus.

- Adding quotes around menu items resulted in a significant drop of the automatic scores, so it was not used; this needs to be further evaluated, as references do not use quotes for menu items either. Nevertheless, quotes were not always useful due to an occasional erroneous identification of menu item boundaries.
- Separate translation of the menu items (sepMenus) gives a positive result of about 0.46 BLEU and 0.63 METEOR.
- Normalizing punctuation (normPunct) has a slightly positive effect when the menu items are translated separately by Lucy.
- Passing only RBMT's unknown words (unk) to SMT results in a loss of 0.4 BLEU.
- Translating the RBMT's menus with SMT (SMTmenus) also deteriorates the scores and
- translating both menu items and unknown words with SMT (unk+SMTmenus) has a positive effect against the baseline and it seems to be comparable with the best system without SMT (sepMenus+normPunct).

2.3 Neural MT system

Our Neural MT algorithms follow the description of Bahdanau et al. (2014). The input sequence is processed using a bidirectional RNN encoder with gated recurrent units (GRU) (Cho et al., 2014) into a sequence of hidden states. The final backward state of the encoder is then projected and used as the initial state of the decoder. Again, our decoder is composed of an RNN with GRU units. In each step, the decoder takes its hidden state and the attention vector (a weighted sum of the hidden states of the encoder, computed separately in each decoding step), and produces the next output word.

In addition to the attention model, we use byte pair encoding (Sennrich et al., 2015) in the preprocessing step. This ensures that there are no out-of-vocabulary words in the corpus and, at the same time, enables for open-vocabulary decoding.

We trained our model on the same data as the PBMT baseline system. We used Batch 1 for validation during the training. In the experiments, the sentence length was limited to 50 tokens. The size of the hidden state of the encoder was 300 units, and the size of the hidden state of the decoder was 256 units. Both source and target word embedding vectors had 300 dimensions. For training, a batch size of 64 sentences was used. We used dropout and L2 for regularization.

Our model was implemented using Neural Monkey,[4] a sequence to sequence learning toolkit built on top of the Tensorflow framework (Abadi et al., 2016). This toolkit was used before by Libovický et al. (2016) in the submission of WMT-2016's multimodal translation and automatic post-editing tasks.

2.4 Selection mechanism

The three systems above are combined with a selection on the sentence level. For every source sentence, the output of every available system is analyzed with several automatic NLP techniques to produce numerical values which indicate some aspects of quality. Out of the numerical values, we form one feature vector which represents the qualitative characteristics of every produced translation output. Consequently, we employ an empirical mechanism which aims to *rank* and *select* given these feature vectors.

The core of the selection mechanism is a ranker which reproduces ranking by aggregating pairwise decisions by a binary classifier (Avramidis, 2013). Such a classifier is trained on binary comparisons in order to select the best one out of two different MT outputs given one source sentence at a time. As training material, we use the test-sets of WMT evaluation task (2008-2014). The rank labels for the training are given by human annotators, as part of the WMT evaluation campaign. The binary comparisons are aggregated per system and the winner is the system which wins the most pairwise comparisons. In order to eliminate cases where two systems win an equal number of pairwise comparison, we weigh each pairwise comparison with its confidence score (soft pairwise recomposition) (Avramidis, 2013).

[4] `http://github.com/ufal/neuralmonkey`

We exhaustively tested the available feature vectors with many machine learning methods including Naïve Bayes, k-nearest Neighbors, Logistic Regression, Linear Discriminant Analysis, Extremely Randomized Trees, Random Tree Forests, Bagging Classifiers, AdaBoost and Gradient Boosting. The models produced were scored in terms of correlation with the original human ranks with Kendall's tau. The scoring was performed on a cross-validation with 10 folds over the entire amount of WMT data. The best correlation was given with Gradient Boosting over an ensemble of 100 single Decision Tree classifiers.

The feature vector consists of 56 distinct features including:

- **Parse probabilities**: the number of feasible k-best parse trees, the highest and the lowest probability in the k-best parse tree list, the mean and the standard deviation of the parse probabilities in the k-best parse tree list,
- **Parse nodes**: the distance of main and subordinate VPs from the end of the target sentence, the count and the average position of nouns in the sentence, the count and the standard deviation of the positions of NPs, PPs and VPs in the sentence, the average and maximum height of VPs in the parse tree, count of target NPs aligned with source NPs via IBM model 1,
- **Punctuation and case**: count, average position and standard deviation of commas, count of dots, uppercase sentence start,
- **Contrastive scores**: BLEU and METEOR using the other two systems as references,
- **Language modeling**: 5-gram language model probability,
- **IBM model 1**: the IBM model 1 scores on both directions, and their ratios, thresholded by either 0.01 and 0.2,
- **Baseline features**: the baseline features of WMT12.

All features can be reproduced using the tool Qualitative (Avramidis, 2016).

3 Evaluation

As mentioned earlier, the hybrid system is developed and tested on a technical domain. All results following are done on the second batch of the QTLeap corpus.

3.1 Automatic evaluation results

Table 3 shows BLEU scores for the systems that we finally chose to feed into our selection mechanism. As reference, we also show scores for the baseline phrase-based SMT system without any of improvements described above. For evaluation, we have used MTComparEval (Klejch et al., 2015). While BLEU scores suggest that both statistical systems are clearly outperforming the RBMT system and also the selection mechanism, inspection of examples did not show such a clear picture.

	BLEU
PB-SMT	37.43
RBMT-baseline	26.96
RBMT-improved	27.53
Neural MT	39.02
Selection mechanism	31.03

Table 3: Automatic scores of the independent components and the selection mechanism

In order to get more insights into the strengths and weaknesses of the systems, we performed a more systematic and detailed manual error analysis on the results.

3.2 Manual evaluation

In context of the QT21 project[5], we have constructed an expansive test suite containing a wide range of various linguistic phenomena that provides a basis for manual analyses in different contexts. Depending on the focus of a manual inspection, different subsections of the test suite can be used to test and evaluate systems. Inspired by the performance of the systems reported here on the test suite, we have constructed a domain-specific test suite based on examples from the QTLeap corpus that represent interesting linguistic phenomena.

The "linguistic phenomena" are understood in a pragmatic sense and cover various aspects that influence the translation quality. Therefore, our phenomena include morpho-syntactic and semantic categories as well as formatting issues, issues of style, etc.

3.3 Manual evaluation methodology

Starting from our evaluation in our contribution to the WMT2016 IT task (Avramidis et al., 2016), we have by now developed an efficient manual evaluation process, performed by a professional German linguist. This procedure consists of the following steps:

1. The linguist has a close look at the output of the different MT systems and identifies systematically occurring translation errors that are related to linguistic phenomena.

2. For each of these linguistic phenomena that seem to be prone to translation errors, 100 segments containing the phenomenon in the source language are extracted, as inspecting the complete test set would be too time-consuming.

3. For each phenomenon, the total occurrences in the source language are counted.

4. Consequently, the total occurrences in the outputs of the different MT systems are counted.

5. The accuracy of the MT outputs for the phenomena is measured by dividing the overall number of correctly translated instances by the overall number of instances in the source segments.

The phenomena that we found to be prone to translation errors in this context were **imperatives**, **compounds**, **menu item separators** (separated by ">"), **quotation marks**, **verbs**, **phrasal verbs** and **terminology**.

As there may always be several correct translations, an occurrence of a phenomenon is not only counted as correctly translated when it matches the reference translation but also when it is for example realized in a different structure that correctly translates the meaning. The following examples demonstrate the manual evaluation technique:

(1)	source:	Yes, type, for example: 50 miles in km.	*1 inst.*
	PB-SMT:	Ja, Typ, zum Beispiel, 50 Meilen in km.	*0 inst.*
	neural:	Ja, Typ, beispielsweise: 50 Meilen in km.	*0 inst.*
	RBMT-imp.:	Tippen Sie zum Beispiel, ja: 50 Meilen in km.	*1 inst.*
	reference:	Ja, geben Sie, zum Beispiel: 50 Meilen in km ein.	

In example 1, the source segment contains one imperative: "type". A correct German translation needs to have the right verb from + the personal pronoun "Sie" in this context. In most of the cases, the imperative "type" is mistranslated as the German noun "Typ" instead of the verb "tippen" or "eingeben", e.g., in the PB-SMT and neural output. The improved RBMT system on the other hand correctly translates the imperative. Note that the reference translation contains the phrasal verb "eingeben" and due to the imperative construction the suffix "ein" moves to the end of the sentence.

[5] www.qt21.eu

(2)	source:	[...] Adjustments ≥ Notification Center ≥ Mail.	*2 inst.*
	PB-SMT:	[...] Adjustments>-Benachrichtigungszentrale ≥ E-Mail.	*1 inst.*
	RBMT:	[...] Anpassungs->-Benachrichtigungs-Zentrums->-Post [...].	*0 inst.*
	RBMT-imp.:	[...] Anpassungen ≥ Benachrichtiungs-Zentrum ≥ Post [...].	*2 inst.*
	reference:	[...] Anpassungen ≥ Benachrichtigungszentrum ≥ Post [...].	

Example 2 depicts the analysis of the menu item separators. The source contains two instances. The PB-SMT output treats the words before and after the first separator as a compound, adding a hyphen after the separator. Therefore, only the second separator counts as correct. The RBMT treats the separators similarly, adding hyphens before and behind the separators, resulting in no correct instances. The improved RBMT version treats all separators correctly.

3.4 Manual evaluation results

The manual evaluation for the paper at hand includes the five systems described above: PB-SMT, RBMT, RBMT-improved, the neural system and the selection mechanism. For the aforementioned seven linguistic phenomena, 657 source segments were extracted[6]. In those 657 source segments, 2105 instances of the different phenomena were found overall, as it was often the case that more than one instance occurred per segment. The results appear in table 4.

	#	PB-SMT	RBMT	RBMT improved	neural	sel. mech.
imperatives	247	68%	79%	**79%**	74%	*73%
compounds	219	55%	87%	**85%**	51%	70%
">" separators	148	**99%**	39%	83%	93%	80%
quotation marks	431	**97%**	94%	75%	95%	80%
verbs	505	85%	93%	**93%**	90%	*90%
phrasal verbs	90	22%	68%	**77%**	38%	53%
terminology	465	**64%**	50%	53%	55%	54%
sum	2105					
average		76%	77%	77%	75%	74%

Table 4: Translation accuracy on manually evaluated sentences focusing on particular phenomena. Test-sets consist of hand-picked source sentences that include the respective phenomenon. Simple RBMT is separated as it does not participate in the selection mechanism. The percentage of the best system in each category is bold-faced, whereas (*) indicates that there is no significant difference ($\alpha = 0.05$) between the selection mechanism and the best system.

As it can be seen in the table, the overall average performance of the components is very similar with no statistically significant difference. The phrase-based SMT and the RBMT system have the highest overall average scores but interestingly their performances on the different linguistic phenomena are quite complimentary:

While the baseline **PB-SMT** system operates best of all systems on the menu item separators (">"), the quotation marks and terminology, the baseline **RBMT** system performs best on the remaining linguistic categories, namely the imperatives, compounds, verbs and phrasal verbs, as well as the quotation marks. The PB-SMT system is furthermore doing well on imperatives and verbs but it has the lowest score of all systems regarding the phrasal verbs. The RBMT system on the other hand also reaches a high score for the quotation marks but has the lowest scores for the menu item separators.

The improved version of the RBMT system, namely the **RBMT-improved**, has the same performance in the overall average compared to its base system. Likewise, it ranks among the best-performing systems

[6]Despite the goal of collecting 100 segments per category, it was only possible to find 57 segments with phrasal verbs.

in terms of imperatives, compounds, verbs and phrasal verbs. Furthermore, it significantly improved on the category it was developed for, i.e. the menu item separator ">". At the same time it has visibly lower scores for the quotation marks (as a side effect of the improved treatment of menu items, the treatment of quotation marks is much worse than for the RBMT baseline system).

The **neural** system reaches a slightly lower score than the other systems. It ranks among the best systems regarding the imperatives, quotation marks and verbs. Furthermore it also shows high scores for the menu item separators. Its score for the compounds on the other hand is the lowest of all systems, close to that of the phrase-based SMT.

The **selection mechanism** obtains the lowest average value of all systems but this score is only three percentage points less than the highest average value. The selection mechanism is one of the best performing systems on imperatives and verbs. For the other phenomena it mostly reaches a score that is lower than the scores of its component systems.

4 Discussion and further work

In this paper, we have presented a hybrid machine translation architecture for German that is based on three different MT engines (phrase-based SMT, RBMT, neural) that are joined by a selection mechanism that uses deep linguistic features among other things.

In terms of evaluation, we have also taken a "deep" approach by integrating a linguist who evaluated the systems' errors on a kind of test suite made of relevant examples representing seven selected "error categories" such as imperatives or terminology. While overall automatic BLEU results indicate that the systems differ in performance (statistical systems outperform the selection mechanism who outperforms the rule-based system), the detailed error evaluation on segment basis has shown a different picture. Looking at the bottom line, i.e., the sum of selected error categories, it seems that all systems perform alike: they all get about 75% of the examples ("error triggers") right. But if we look at the detailed distribution, it turns out that the systems perform significantly different on the different categories.

While the selection mechanism was the best performing system in terms of errors in previous work (Avramidis et al., 2016), it was not able to reduce some of the errors in the given experiments. This is not surprising as the error categories shown here are not explicitly handled by the selection mechanism. Additionally, whereas the performance is measured on a domain-specific test-set, the selection mechanism was trained on generic news corpora, for lack of in-domain annotations. As future work, one option would be to explicitly handle the errors, e.g., by including features into the selection mechanism that trigger certain action if, say, an imperative is detected. Likewise, this error-driven type of evaluation can also be used to improve the data-driven engines, e.g., by creating special corpora for selected phenomena.

Whenever dealing with language, it is clear that phenomena do not act independently, thus it is not surprising that the improvement of one phenomenon may have side effects on the other phenomena (as it was the case with Lucy-improved). For future work, we plan to partly automate our test suites in order to be able to track the effects of improving the systems. For the time being, this can also be realized by manual inspection with certain intermediate steps.

One notable insight of the experiments presented here and also from further inspection of examples is that the neural system does not seem to be able to take advantage of the (technical) domain data in the training data as compared to phrase-based SMT. This might explain why the neural system does not massively outperform phrase-based SMT here as it has been seen in other contexts cited above.

Acknowledgments

This work has received support from the ECs FP7 (FP7/2007-2013) under grant agreement number 610516 (QTLeap) and from the ECs Horizon 2020 research and innovation programme under grant agreement number 645452 (QT21).

References

Martin Abadi, Ashish Agarwal, Paul Barham, Eugene Brevdo, Zhifeng Chen, Craig Citro, Greg S Corrado, Andy Davis, Jeffrey Dean, Matthieu Devin, and Others. 2016. Tensorflow: Large-scale machine learning on heterogeneous distributed systems. *arXiv preprint arXiv:1603.04467.*

Juan A Alonso and Gregor Thurmair. 2003. The Comprendium Translator system. In *Proceedings of the Ninth Machine Translation Summit.* International Association for Machine Translation (IAMT).

Eleftherios Avramidis, Burchardt, Aljoscha, Vivien Macketanz, and Ankit Srivastava. 2016. DFKI's system for WMT16 IT-domain task, including analysis of systematic errors. In *Proceedings of the First Conference on Machine Translation*, pages 415–422, Berlin, Germany, aug. Association for Computational Linguistics.

Eleftherios Avramidis. 2013. Sentence-level ranking with quality estimation. *Machine Translation*, 27(Special issue on Quality Estimation):239–256.

Eleftherios Avramidis. 2016. Qualitative: Python Tool for MT Quality Estimation Supporting Server Mode and Hybrid MT. *The Prague Bulletin of Mathematical Linguistics (PBML)*, 106:147–158.

Dzmitry Bahdanau, Kyunghyun Cho, and Yoshua Bengio. 2014. Neural {Machine} {Translation} by {Jointly} {Learning} to {Align} and {Translate}. *arXiv:1409.0473 [cs, stat]*, sep.

Ondej Bojar, Rajen Chatterjee, Christian Federmann, Yvette Graham, Barry Haddow, Matthias Huck, Antonio Jimeno Yepes, Philipp Koehn, Varvara Logacheva, Christof Monz, Matteo Negri, Aurelie Neveol, Mariana Neves, Martin Popel, Matt Post, Raphael Rubino, Carolina Scarton, Lucia Specia, Marco Turchi, Karin Verspoor, and Marcos Zampieri. 2016. Findings of the 2016 Conference on Machine Translation. In *Proceedings of the First Conference on Machine Translation*, pages 131–198, Berlin, Germany, aug. Association for Computational Linguistics.

Aljoscha Burchardt, Kim Harris, Georg Rehm, and Hans Uszkoreit. 2016a. Towards a systematic and human-informed paradigm for high-quality machine translation. In Georg Rehm, Aljoscha Burchardt, Ondrej Bojar, Christian Dugast, Marcello Federico, Josef van Genabith, Barry Haddow, Jan Haji, Kim Harris, Philipp Khn, Matteo Negri, Martin Popel, Lucia Specia, Marco Turchi, and Hans Uszkoreit, editors, *Proceedings of the LREC 2016 Workshop Translation Evaluation: From Fragmented Tools and Data Sets to an Integrated Ecosystem*, pages 35–42, Portoro, Slovenia, May.

Aljoscha Burchardt, Kim Harris, Georg Rehm, and Hans Uszkoreit. 2016b. Towards a Systematic and Human-Informed Paradigm for High-Quality Machine Translation. In Georg Rehm, Aljoscha Burchardt, Ondrej Bojar, Christian Dugast, Marcello Federico, Josef van Genabith, Barry Haddow, Jan Hajic, Kim Harris, Philipp Koehn, Matteo Negri, Martin Popel, Lucia Specia, Marco Turchi, and Hans Uszkoreit, editors, *Proceedings of the LREC 2016 Workshop "Translation Evaluation: From Fragmented Tools and Data Sets to an Integrated Ecosystem". Translation Evaluation: From Fragmented Tools and Data Sets to an Integrated Ecosystem (LREC-2016), located at International Co.* o.A.

Chris Callison-Burch, Cameron Fordyce, Philipp Koehn, Christof Monz, and Josh Schroeder. 2007. (Meta-) evaluation of machine translation. In *Proceedings of the Second Workshop on Statistical Machine Translation (StatMT'07)*, pages 136–158, Prague, Czech Republic, jun. Association for Computational Linguistics.

Kyunghyun Cho, Bart van Merrienboer, Dzmitry Bahdanau, and Yoshua Bengio. 2014. On the Properties of Neural Machine Translation: Encoder–Decoder Approaches. In *Proceedings of SSST-8, Eighth Workshop on Syntax, Semantics and Structure in Statistical Translation*, pages 103–111, Doha, Qatar, oct. Association for Computational Linguistics.

Kenneth Heafield. 2011. KenLM : Faster and Smaller Language Model Queries. In *Proceedings of the Sixth Workshop on Statistical Machine Translation*, number 2009, pages 187–197, Edinburgh, Scotland, jul. Association for Computational Linguistics.

Ondrej Klejch, Eleftherios Avramidis, Aljoscha Burchardt, and Martin Popel. 2015. MT-ComparEval: Graphical evaluation interface for Machine Translation development. *The Prague Bulletin of Mathematical Linguistics*, 104(1):63–74.

Philipp Koehn, Abhishek Arun, and Hieu Hoang. 2008. Towards better Machine Translation Quality for the German-English Language Pairs. In *Proceedings of the Third Workshop on Statistical Machine Translation*, pages 139–142, Columbus, Ohio, jun. Association for Computational Linguistics.

Philipp Koehn. 2010. An Experimental Management System. *The Prague Bulletin of Mathematical Linguistics*, 94(-1):87–96.

Jindich Libovický, Jindich Helcl, Marek Tlustý, Pavel Pecina, and Ondej Bojar. 2016. CUNI System for WMT16 Automatic Post-Editing and Multimodal Translation Tasks. *CoRR*, abs/1606.0.

Franz Josef Och. 2003. Minimum error rate training in statistical machine translation. In *ACL '03: Proceedings of the 41st Annual Meeting on Association for Computational Linguistics*, pages 160–167, Morristown, NJ, USA. Association for Computational Linguistics.

Holger Schwenk and Philipp Koehn. 2008. Large and Diverse Language Models for Statistical Machine Translation. In *Proceedings of the Third International Joint Conference on Natural Language Processing: Volume-II*.

Rico Sennrich, Barry Haddow, and Alexandra Birch. 2015. Neural Machine Translation of Rare Words with Subword Units. *CoRR*, abs/1508.0.

Andreas Stolcke. 2002. SRILM an Extensible Language Modeling Toolkit. In *System*, volume 2, pages 901–904. ISCA, sep.

Adding syntactic structure to bilingual terminology for improved domain adaptation

Mikel Artetxe[1], Gorka Labaka[1], Chakaveh Saedi[2], João Rodrigues[2], João Silva[2], António Branco[2], Eneko Agirre[1]
[1] IXA Group, Faculty of Computer Science, University of the Basque Country, Spain
[2] Department of Informatics, Faculty of Sciences, University of Lisbon, Portugal
[1] {mikel.artexe, gorka.labaka, e.agirre}@ehu.eus,
[2] {chakaveh.saedi, joao.rodrigues, jsilva, antonio.branco}@di.fc.ul.pt

Abstract

Deep-syntax approaches to machine translation have emerged as an alternative to phrase-based statistical systems. TectoMT is an open source framework for transfer-based MT which works at the deep tectogrammatical level and combines linguistic knowledge and statistical techniques. When adapting to a domain, terminological resources improve results with simple techniques, e.g. force-translating domain-specific expressions. In such approaches, multiword entries are translated as if they were a single token-with-spaces, failing to represent the internal structure which makes TectoMT a powerful translation engine. In this work we enrich source and target multiword terms with syntactic structure, and seamlessly integrate them in the tree-based transfer phase of TectoMT. Our experiments on the IT domain using the Microsoft terminological resource show improvement in Spanish, Basque and Portuguese.

1 Introduction

TectoMT (Žabokrtský et al., 2008; Popel and Žabokrtský, 2010) has emerged as an architecture to develop deep-transfer systems, where the translation step is done a deep level of analysis, in contrast to methods based on surface sequences of words. TectoMT combines linguistic knowledge and statistical techniques, particularly during transfer, and it aims at transfer on the so-called tectogrammatical layer (Hajičová, 2000), a layer of deep syntactic dependency trees.

In domain adaptation of machine translation, a typical scenario is as follows: there is an MT system trained on large general-domain data, and there is a bilingual terminological resource which covers part of the vocabulary of the target domain. In this case, a simple force-translate approach can suffice to obtain good results (Dušek et al., 2015). In the context of TectoMT, this approach is implemented identifying source terms in the analysis phase, and adding as a single node in the tree. In the case of multiword terms, this means that the internal structure is not captured and that it is not possible to access the internal morphological and syntactic information.

In this work we enrich source and target multiword terms with syntactic structure (so-called "treelets"), and seamlessly integrate them in the tree-based transfer phase of TectoMT. This allows to check for morphological agreement when producing translation (e.g. gender of noun-adjective terms in Spanish). The results on three languages within the Information Technology (IT) domain show consistent improvements when applied on the Microsoft terminological resource.

2 TectoMT

As most rule-based systems, TectoMT consists of analysis, transfer and synthesis stages. It works on different levels of abstraction up to the tectogrammatical level (cf. Figure 1) and uses *blocks* and *scenarios* to process the information across the architecture (see below).

2.1 Tecto layers

TectoMT works on an stratified approach to language, that is, it defines four layers in increasing level of abstraction: raw text (w-layer), morphological layer (m-layer), shallow-syntax layer (a-layer), and

Proceedings of the 2nd Deep Machine Translation Workshop (DMTW 2016), pages 39–46,
Lisbon, Portugal, 21 October 2016.

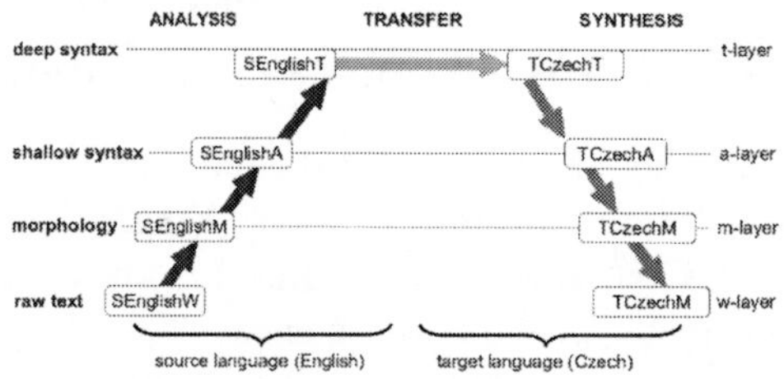

Figure 1: The general TectoMT architecture (from Popel and Žabokrtský (2010:298)).

deep-syntax layer (t-layer). This strategy is adopted from the Functional Generative Description theory (Sgall, 1967), further elaborated and implemented in the Prague Dependency Treebank (PDT) (Hajič et al., 2006). As explained by Popel and Žabokrtský (2010:296), each layer contains the following representations (see Figure 2):

Morphological layer (m-layer) Each sentence is tokenized and tokens are annotated with a lemma and morphological tag, e.g. *did: do-VBD.*

Analytical layer (a-layer) Each sentence is represented as a shallow-syntax dependency tree (a-tree), with a 1-to-1 correspondence between m-layer tokens and a-layer nodes. Each a-node is annotated with the type of dependency relation to its governing node, e.g. *did* is a dependent of *tell (VB)* with a *AuxV* relation type.

Tectogrammatical layer (t-layer) Each sentence is represented as a deep-syntax dependency tree (t-tree) where lexical words are represented as t-layer nodes, and the meaning conveyed by function words (auxiliary verbs, prepositions and subordinating conjunctions, etc.) is represented in t-node attributes, e.g. *did* is no longer a separate node but part of the lexical verb-node *tell*. The most important attributes of t-nodes are:

tectogrammatical lemma;

functor the semantic value of syntactic dependency relations, e.g. actor, effect, causal adjuncts;

grammatemes semantically oriented counterparts of morphological categories at the highest level of abstraction, e.g. tense, number, verb modality, negation;

formeme the morphosyntactic form of a t-node in the surface sentence. The set of formeme values depends on its semantic part of speech, e.g. noun as subject (n:subj), noun as direct object (n:obj), noun within a prepositional phrase (n:*in*+X) (Dušek et al., 2012).

2.2 The TectoMT system

TectoMT is integrated in Treex,[1] a modular open-source NLP framework. Blocks are independent components of sequential steps into which NLP tasks can be decomposed. Each block has a well-defined input/output specification and, usually, a linguistically interpretable functionality. Blocks are reusable and can be listed as part of different task sequences. We call these *scenarios*.

TectoMT includes over 1,000 blocks; approximately 224 English-specific blocks, 237 for Czech, over 57 for English-to-Czech transfer, 129 for other languages and 467 language-independent blocks.[2] Blocks vary in length, as they can consist of a few lines of code or tackle complex linguistic phenomena.

3 Terminology as Gazetteers

The easiest form to exploit domain terminology is to use them as fixed translation units, where the term needs to appear in the source text in a fixed inflectional form. That is, if the form appears in

[1] `https://ufal.mff.cuni.cz/treex`

[2] Statistics taken from: `https://github.com/ufal/treex.git` (27/08/2015)

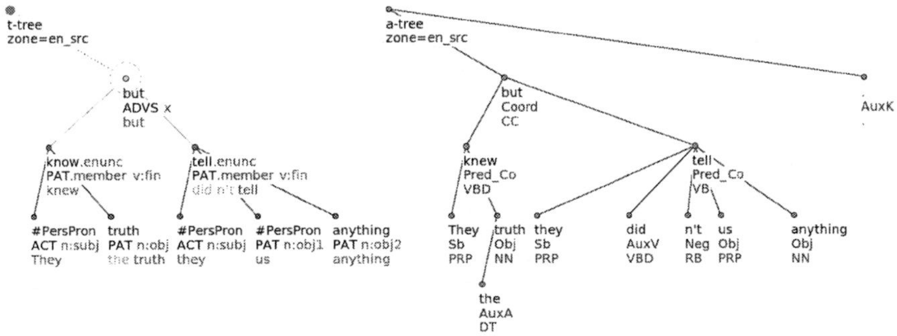

Figure 2: a-level and t-level English analysis of the sentence "`They knew the truth but they didn't tell us anything.`"

English		Spanish	
`liboff_1`	`Accessories`	`liboff_1`	`Accesorios`
`liboff_2`	`Start at`	`liboff_2`	`Empezar en`
`kde_1`	`Programs`	`kde_1`	`Programas`
`kde_2`	`System tools`	`kde_2`	`Herramientas del sistema`
`kde_3`	`Start`	`kde_3`	`Iniciar`
`kde_4`	`Disk`	`kde_4`	`Disco`
`kde_5`	`PC running on low battery`	`kde_5`	`Equipo funcionando bajo de bateria`
`kde_6`	`System`	`kde_6`	`Systema`
`kde_7`	`Start`	`kde_7`	`Comenzar`
`wiki_1`	`PC`	`wiki_1`	`PC`

Figure 3: A sample of English-Spanish terminological resources from localization files.

some inflected form which is not present in the dictionary, it is not translated. Given that terminological resources contain mainly base forms, several terms are missed in the source texts. The property of having a fixed form allows for easy implementation: match the source expression in the terminological resource in the source text and replace it deterministically by its equivalent.

In this work we are interested in the IT domain, concerning software texts which includes, among other, menu items, button names, sequences of those and system messages.

3.1 Lexicon collection and format

The straightforward way to obtain terminology resources is to extract them from freely available software localization files. We designed a general extractor that accepts `.po` localization files and outputs a lexicon. The lexicon is formed by two lists containing corresponding expressions in two languages. Each of the two lists consist of two columns: a unique expression identifier, the expression itself. The identifier is the same for equivalent terms. Figure 3 shows an excerpt from an English-Spanish gazetteer.

3.2 Translation method

Translation using gazetteers proceeds in multiple steps:

Matching the lexicon items. This is the most complex stage of the whole process. It is performed just after the tokenization, before any linguistic processing is conducted. Lexicon items are matched in the source tokenized text and the matched items, which can possibly span several neighboring tokens, are replaced by a single-word placeholder.

In the initialization stage, the source language part of the lexicon is loaded and structured in a word-based trie to reduce time complexity of the text search. In the current implementation, if an expression appears more than once in the source gazetteer list, only its first occurrence is stored. Therefore, the performance of gazetteer matching machinery depends on the ordering of the gazetteer lists. A trie built

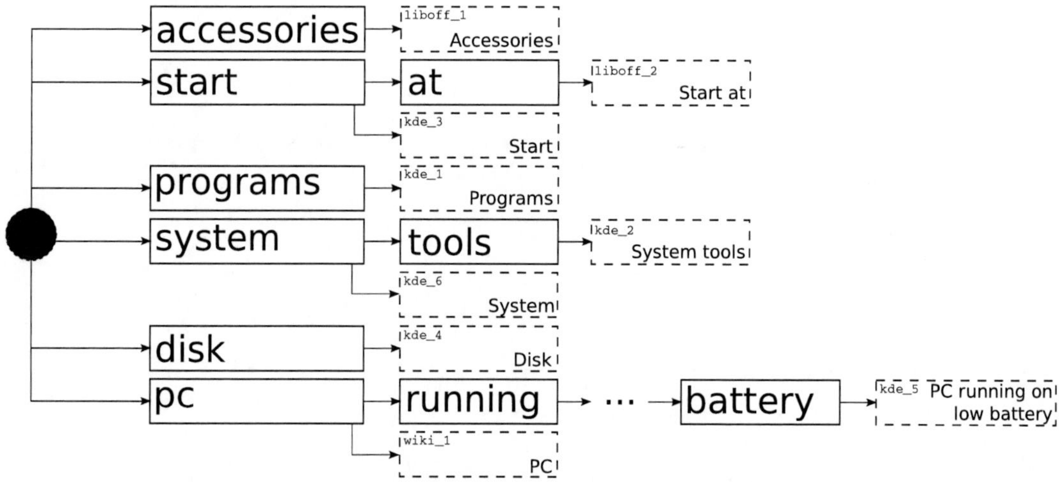

Figure 4: A trie created from the English terms in Figure 3

from the English list of the sample English-Spanish gazetteer is depicted in Figure 4. Note that the kde_7 item is not represented in the trie, since the slot is already occupied by the kde_3 item.

The trie is then used to match the expressions in the list to the source text. The matched expressions might overlap. A scoring function estimates whether the term is actually a term in the text. Thus, every matched expression is assigned a score. entity. Figure 5 shows a sample sentence (a), including matched expressions and scores assigned (b). The matches with positive score are ordered by the score and filtered to get non-overlapping matches, taking those with higher score first. The matched words belonging to a single term are then replaced by a single placeholder word (see Figure 5c).

As a last step, the neighboring terms are collapsed into one and replaced by the placeholder word. As a heuristic for the IT domain, terms that occur separated by a $>$ symbol are also collapsed. This measure is aimed at translation of menu items and button labels sequences, which frequently appear in the IT domain corpus. After this step, the sample sentence becomes drastically simplified, which should be much easier to process by a part-of-speech tagger and parser (see Figure 5e). However, all the information necessary to reconstruct the original expressions or their lexicon translations are stored (see Figure 5d).

Translating matched items. The expressions matched in the source language are transferred over the tectogrammatical layer to the target language. Here, the placeholder words are substituted by the expressions from the target language list of the gazetteer, which are looked up using the identifiers coupled with the placeholder words. Possible delimiters are retained. This is performed before any other words are translated. The tectogrammatical representation of the simplified sample English sentence (Figure 5d) is transferred to Spanish by translating the gazetteer matches first, followed by the standard TetoMT steps (lexical choice for the other words and concluded with the synthesis stage, cf. Figure 5g).

4 Terminology as treelets

As shown in the previous section, simple string matching with gazetteers is appropriate to translate fixed terms in the IT domain like menu items, button names and system messages. However, this technique has two important limitations when applied to terminology other than those fixes terms, including common nouns (driver, file...) or verbs (run, set up...):

1. It does not handle inflection, neither in the source language nor in the target language, so the different surface forms of a given term (e.g. run, runs, running, ran) will not be translated unless there is a separate entry for each of them. This is particularly relevant for morphologically rich languages like Spanish (verb inflection) or Basque.

a) To defragment the PC, click Start > Programs > Accessories > System Tools > Disk Defragment.

b) To defragment the [PC wiki_1=24], click [Start kde_3=24] > [Programs kde_1=24] > [Accessories liboff_1=24] > [[System kde_6=24] Tools kde_2=44] > [Disk kde_4=24] Defragment.

c) To defragment the [PH wiki_1], click [PH kde_3] > [PH kde_1] > [PH liboff_1] > [PH kde_2] > [PH kde_4] Defragment.

d) To defragment the [PH wiki_1], click [PH kde_3 > kde_1 > liboff_1 > kde_2 > kde_4] Defragment.

e) To defragment the PH, click PH Defragment.

f) To defragment the [PC wiki_1], click [Comienzo > Programas > Accesorios > Herramientas del sistema > Disco kde_3 > kde_1 > liboff_1 > kde_2 > kde_4] Defragment.

g) Desfragmentador el PC haga clic Iniciar > Programas > Accesorios > Herramientas del Sistema > Disco desfragmentador.

Figure 5: A sample English sentence processed by the English-Spanish gazetteer. Translation process is shown step by step. See text for details. PH stands for placeholder

2. It does not handle morphosyntactic ambiguity. For instance, the English term "test" can either be a noun or a verb, and its translation depends on that.

In order to overcome these issues, we developed a terminology translation module which is applied on the t-layer. The translation process involves the following steps:

1. **Preprocessing:** The terminology dictionary is first preprocessed so it can be efficiently used later at runtime. For that purpose, the lemma of each entry in the dictionary is independently analyzed up to the t-layer in both languages. This analysis is done without any context, so if there is some ambiguity, it might happen that the analysis given by the system does not match the sense it has in the dictionary. For instance, the English term 'file' might be analyzed either as a verb or a noun, but its entry in the dictionary and, consequently, its translation, will correspond to only one of these senses. For that reason, we decide to remove all entries whose part-of-speech tag in the original dictionary does not match the one assigned to the root node by the analyzer.

2. **Matching:** During this stage, we search for occurrences of the dictionary entries in the text to translate, which is done at the t-layer. For that purpose, the preprocessed tree of a term is considered to match a subtree of the text to translate if the lemma and part-of-speech tag of their root node are the same and their corresponding children nodes recursively match for all their attributes. By limiting the matching criteria of the root node to the lemma and part-of-speech, the system is able to match different surface forms of a single entry (e.g. "local area network" and "local area networks"). Note that, thanks to the deep representation used at the t-layer, we are also able to capture form variations in tokens other than the root. For instance, in Spanish both adjectives and nouns carry gender and number information, but in the t-layer only the highest node encodes this information. This way, the system will be able to match both "disco duro" ("hard disk") and "discos duros" ("hard disks") for a single dictionary entry, even if the surface form of the children node "duro" was not the same in the original text. In addition to that, it should be noted that we do allow the subtree of the text to translate to have additional children nodes to the left or right, but only at the

	en-eu	en-es	en-pt
KDE	70,298	98,510	98,505
LibreOffice	70,991	75,482	75,743
VLC	5,548	6,214	6,215
Wikipedia	1,505	24,610	20,239
Total Localization	148,342	204,816	200,702
Microsoft Terminology	6,474	25,069	15,748

Table 1: Source and number of gazetteer entries in each language.

first level below the root node, so we are able to match chunks like "corporate local area network" or "external hard disk" for the previous examples.

In order to do the matching efficiently, we use a prebuilt hash table that maps the lemma and part-of-speech pair of the root node of each dictionary entry to the full tree obtained in the preprocessing stage. This way, for each node in the input tree, we look up its lemma and part-of-speech in this hash map and, for all the occurrences, recursively check if their children nodes match.

3. **Translation:** During translation, we replace each matched subtree with the tree of its corresponding translation in the dictionary, which was built in the preprocessing stage. For that purpose, the children nodes of the matched subtree are simply removed and the ones from the dictionary are inserted in their place. As for the root node, the lemma and part-of-speech are replaced with the one from the dictionary, but all the other attributes are left unchanged. Given that these attributes are language independent, the appropriate surface form will then be generated in subsequent stages, so for our example "local area network" is translated as "red de area local" while "local area networks" is translated as "redes de area local", even if there is a single entry for them in the dictionary.

5 Experiments

We conducted experiments in three languages, using English as the source language. The experiments were carried on an IT dataset released by the QTLeap project.[3] The systems were trained in publicly available corpora, mostly Europarl, with the exception of Basque, where we used an in-house corpus for training.

Localization Gazetteers The gazetteers for Basque, Spanish and Portuguese were collected from four different sources: the localization files of VLC,[4] LibreOffice,[5] and KDE[6]; and IT-related Wikipedia articles. In addition, some manual filtering (blacklisting) was performed on all the gazetteers.

For mining IT-related terms from Wikipedia, we adopted the method by Gaudio and Branco (2012). This method exploits the hierarchical structure of Wikipedia articles. This structure allows for extracting articles on specific topics, selecting the articles directly linked to a superordinate category. For this purpose, Wikipedia dumps from June 2015 were used for each of the languages, and they were accessed using the Java Wikipedia Library, an open-source, Java-based application programming interface that allows to access all information contained in Wikipedia (Zesch et al., 2008). Using as starting point the most generic categories in the IT field, all the articles linked to these categories and their children were selected. The titles of these article were used as entries in the gazetteers. The inter-language links were used to translate the title in the original languages to English. Similar result could be expected if the method was applied to the Linked Open Data version of Wikipedia, DBPedia,

[3]More specifically on the Batch2 answer corpus

[4]`http://downloads.videolan.org/pub/videolan/vlc/2.1.5/vlc-2.1.5.tar.xz`

[5]`http://download.documentfoundation.org/libreoffice/src/4.4.0/libreoffice-translations-4.4.0.3.tar.xz`

[6]`svn://anonsvn.kde.org/home/kde/branches/stable/l10n-kde4/{es,eu,pt}/messages`

	en→es
TectoMT	29.60
+Gazetteers	32.01
+Gazetteers+Msoft$_{Gazetteer}$	32.25
+Gazetteers+Msoft$_{Treelet}$	34.16

Table 2: BLEU scores for Spanish

	en→eu	en→pt
TectoMT	17.15	21.96
+Gazetteers	20.51	22.68
+Gazetteers+Msoft$_{Treelet}$	23.41	23.01

Table 3: BLEU scores for Basque and Portuguese

The figures of collected gazetteer entries for all the sources are presented in Table 1. The gazetteers have been released through Meta-Share.[7]

Microsoft Terminology Collection The Microsoft Terminology Collection is publicly available for nearly 100 languages[8]. It uses the standard TermBase eXchange (TBX) format and, for each entry, it includes the English lemma, the target language lemma, their part-of-speech in both language, and a brief definition in English. Note that the dictionary also includes many multiword terms, such as "local area network" or "single click".

5.1 Results for Spanish

The results in Table 2 show the results of the two baselines: TectoMT without gazetteers and TectoMT with all gazetteers, except the Microsoft gazetteer. When including the Microsoft terminology as a gazetteer, there is a small improvement. When including the Microsoft terminology as treelets, the improvement is larger, up to 34.16.

5.2 Results for Basque and Portuguese

Given the good results, we repeated a similar experiment for Basque and Portuguese (cf. Table 2). We also show the results of the two baselines: TectoMT without gazetteers and TectoMT with all gazetteers, except the Microsoft gazetteer. When including the Microsoft terminology as treelets, we also obtain an improvement in both languages, larger for Basque and smaller for Portuguese.

6 Conclusions

In this paper we present a system for terminology translation based on deep approaches. We analyse the terms in the resource, and integrate them in a deep syntax-based MT engine, TectoMT. Our method is able to translate complex terms exhibiting different morphosyntactic agreement phenomena. The results on the IT domain show that this method is effective for Spanish, Basque and Portuguese when applied on the Microsoft terminological resource. For the future, we would like to extend our approach to the rest of the terminological resources, and to present more experiments and error analysis to show the value of our approach.

Acknowledgements

The research leading to these results has received funding from FP7-ICT-2013-10-610516 (QTLeap) and from P2020-3279 (ASSET).

[7]`http://metashare.metanet4u.eu/go2/qtleap-specialized-lexicons`
[8]`https://www.microsoft.com/Language/en-US/Terminology.aspx`

References

Ondřej Dušek, Zdeněk Žabokrtský, Martin Popel, Martin Majliš, Michal Novák, and David Mareček. 2012. Formemes in English-Czech deep syntactic MT. In *Proceedings of the Seventh Works-hop on Statistical Machine Translation*, pages 267–274. Association for Computational Linguistics.

Ondřej Dušek, Luís Gomes, Michal Novák, Martin Popel, and Rudolf Rosa. 2015. New language pairs in tectomt. In *Proceedings of the Tenth Workshop on Statistical Machine Translation*, pages 98–104, Lisbon, Portugal, September. Association for Computational Linguistics.

Rosa Gaudio and Antonio Branco. 2012. Using wikipedia to collect a corpus for automatic definition extraction: comparing english and portuguese languages. In *Anais do XI Encontro de Linguistiva de Corpus - ELC 2012*, Instituto de Ciłncias Matemticas e de Computao da USP, em So Carlos/SP.

Jan Hajič, Jarmila Panevová, Eva Hajičová, Petr Sgall, Petr Pajas, Jan Štepánek, Jiří Havelka, Marie Mikulová, Zdenek Žabokrtský, and Magda Ševcıková Razımová. 2006. Prague dependency treebank 2.0. *CD-ROM, Linguistic Data Consortium, LDC Catalog No.: LDC2006T01, Philadelphia*, 98.

Eva Hajičová. 2000. Dependency-based underlying-structure tagging of a very large Czech corpus. *TAL. Traitement automatique des langues*, 41(1):57–78.

Martin Popel and Zdeněk Žabokrtský. 2010. TectoMT: modular NLP framework. In *Advances in natural language processing*, pages 293–304. Springer.

Petr Sgall. 1967. Functional sentence perspective in a generative description. *Prague studies in mathematical linguistics*, 2(203-225).

Zdeněk Žabokrtský, Jan Ptáček, and Petr Pajas. 2008. TectoMT: Highly modular MT system with tectogrammatics used as transfer layer. In *Proceedings of the Third Workshop on Statistical Machine Translation*, pages 167–170. Association for Computational Linguistics.

Torsten Zesch, Christof Müller, and Iryna Gurevych. 2008. Extracting Lexical Semantic Knowledge from Wikipedia and Wikictionary. In Nicoletta Calzolari, Khalid Choukri, Bente Maegaard, Joseph Mariani, Jan Odjik, Stelios Piperidis, and Daniel Tapias, editors, *Proceedings of the Sixth International Language Resources and Evaluation (LREC 2008)*, Marrakech, Morocco. European Language Resources Association (ELRA).

Incorporation of a Valency Lexicon into a TectoMT Pipeline

Natalia Klyueva and Vladislav Kuboň

Institute of Formal and Applied Linguistics
Charles University in Prague
E-mail: kljueva,vk@ufal.mff.cuni.cz

Abstract

In this paper, we focus on the incorporation of a valency lexicon into TectoMT system for Czech-Russian language pair. We demonstrate valency errors in MT output and describe how the introduction of a lexicon influenced the translation results. Though there was no impact on BLEU score, the manual inspection of concrete cases showed some improvement.

1 Introduction

The work on Machine Translation systems was traditionally presented as a collaboration between linguists and computer scientists: linguists prepared data (e.g. dictionaries and transfer rules), and computer scientists implemented the baseline of the system. Linguists analyzed the output translations and on the basis of these translations suggested further improvements and then the cycle was repeated.

The interplay between linguistics and computer science as described above was true for rule-based machine translation (RBMT) systems only before the data-driven (statistical, SMT). There was no longer a need for many linguists with the knowledge of the source and the target languages: all the necessary information was acquired from data, the evaluation was done either automatically or manually by native speakers rather than by experts in linguistics.

A big advantage of RBMT systems over SMT is that the former are more controllable and predictable. The errors produced by RBMT are easy to spot and it is often obvious how to fix them (but not always easy) – e.g. by some additional rules.

In this paper, we analyze the output of MT system between Czech and Russian with respect to valency errors. We make an experiment with a rule-based MT system implemented within a framework TectoMT (for other language pairs TectoMT involves statistical methods and modules as well, our implementation of Czech-to-Russian MT system can be considered primarily rule-based) and incorporate a list of surface valency frames into the translation pipeline.

The paper will be structured as follows. In Section 2 we describe theoretical and practical aspects of TectoMT and the implementation of Czech-to-Russian MT. Section 3 presents definition of valency and an overview of a valency resource used in the experiment. In Sections 4 and 5 we describe valency errors in MT output and incorporation of the valency lexicon into a translation pipeline. Manual evaluation of the proposed method is given in Section 6.

2 TectoMT

The TectoMT system between Czech and Russian was implemented within the framework **Treex** (Popel and Žabokrtský, 2009). Treex is a modular system of NLP tools, such as tokenizers, taggers and parsers that were created to process corpora and treebanks in multiple languages. One of the main projects under Treex is the English-Czech machine translation system (Popel,

Proceedings of the 2nd Deep Machine Translation Workshop (DMTW 2016), pages 47–53,
Lisbon, Portugal, 21 October 2016.

2010). Modules of the system are easily reusable for other languages, so in order to build a Czech-Russian MT, a Czech analysis module that was already present in the system was used and the Russian synthesis module was created.

Translation scenario in TectoMT consists of a sequence of **blocks** which ensure the transformation between the four language layers: word, morphological, analytical (shallow syntactic) and tectogrammatical (deep syntactic) layers, plus a scenario for a transfer phase[1]. This division has its roots in the Functional Grammar Description theory – FGD (Sgall et al., 1986), but its implementation in Treex is slightly different from original FGD concepts.

Below, we will provide a description of layers how they are used in Treex/TectoMT.

- **The Word and Morphological Layer.** A sentence represented as a sequence of tokens. On the morphological layer, each token in the sequence is represented as a word form with a lemma and a tag assigned.
- **The Analytical Layer.** Syntactic annotation is presented in the form of a dependency tree, where each morphologically annotated token from the previous level becomes a node with an assigned *analytical function* (**afun**). Analytical function reflects the syntactic relation between a parent and a child node (e.g. Subject, predicate etc.) and is stored as an attribute of the child.
- **The Tectogrammatical Layer**. The annotation on the tectogrammatical layer (t-layer) goes deeper towards the level of meaning. Function words (prepositions, auxiliary verbs etc.) are removed from the corresponding analytical tree; they are stored as attributes of autosemantic words, leaving only content words as the nodes on the t-layer.

Initially, the baseline system was established with a minimum number of rules handling the most obvious differences between the languages, such as copula drop or negation particle handling. The BLEU score (Papineni et al., 2002) of the baseline experiment was poor – 4.44%. We attribute such a low score mainly to the automatically generated dictionary, but also some errors might be introduced by the tagger, the parser and the module of word forms generation.

We included some blocks to fix certain linguistic phenomena: list of prepositions and verbs plus their formemes, copula drop, modal verbs, fixing year construction in Russian and some other minor fixes. The improvement of specific issues in terms of BLEU was very little, but the analysis always showed some improvement in an issue that we aimed for. After applying all those blocks and enlarging the dictionary, the BLEU score reached **9.38%**. We manually explored an MT output, and here we describe one concrete type of MT errors that concerns valency.

3 Valency

The notion of valency itself is not very straightforward and can be understood differently by different researchers. Traditionally, in general linguistics, it is used to indicate that the verb requires some number of complements of a certain semantic type. Here, we will refer to valency with respect to its surface realization – morphemic endings of nouns or preposition required by a verb. So, under the notion 'valency frames' we will understand mainly surface forms of frame elements. In this experiment we focus only on verbal valency though we admit that with nominal valency we face similar challenges as with verbal.

Czech and Russian are related languages, and on the first sight there are not many distinctions in valency. In order to prove this statistically, we computed the number of different valency frames in the two languages. To extract valency frames, we exploit the MT dictionary Ruslan that was created for the experiments in MT between Czech and Russian in 1980s, (Hajic, 1987), (Oliva., 1989).

In the dictionary, verbs were assigned with their valency frames in Czech and the corresponding frames in Russian with the specification of a semantic class of all verb complements. Example

[1]For the transfer we used an automatically extracted Czech-Russian dictionary.

1 demonstrates an entry from Ruslan dictionary for the verb *vystačit* – 'to be enough', the explanatory notes are given further:

(1) VYSTAC3==R(5,PRP,?(N(D),S(I,G)),39,CHVATIT6):

- *VYSTAC3* presents a stem of the verb *vystačit* – 'be enough',
- *R* denotes a root of a tree,
- *5* is a symbol for a verb and PRP is a conjugation pattern of the Czech verb,
- *N(D),S(I,G))* is a valency frame that we will further describe in detail,
- *39* is a Russian declination pattern,
- CHVATIT6 is the Russian translation of a lexeme, coded in Latin

We transformed the entry from the original Ruslan format: lowercased the entries, transferred Ruslan encoding of letters with diacritics (coded in numbers) into common letters, converted Latin into Cyrillic letters for a Russian word. Then we selected the verbs and substituted the verb stem and the morphological information coded in special symbols with an appropriate verb ending. Out of the 2080 verbal dictionary entries from Ruslan we have analyzed 1856 unique verbs. We have divided verbs on the basis whether a verb requires the prepositional case or the non-prepositional one.

Czech and Russian non-prepositional valency slots have usually identical cases, 68 verbs (3.6%) out of all the lexicon have some discrepancy in the frame (e.g., (cz)vyhýbat se + Dat -> (ru) избегать + Gen – *to avoid*). As for the prepositional cases, 104 (5.6 %) of verbs have different surface frames containing prepositions (e.g., (cz)doufat v + Acc -> (ru)надеяться на + Acc – *to believe in*).

The main result of this transformation is a small bilingual lexicon and that is included into a TectoMT translation scenario.

4 Valency errors in MT

We found valency errors to be crucial in MT output: verb and its complements form a core of a sentence, so the mistakes in the surface form of the complements can considerably lower the quality of a sentence. The reasons for errors in valency are twofold. The most evident case is when Russian and Czech valency have some discrepancies, and the Czech structure is used in a Russian output.

In the following example, a Czech verb 'to influence' is governed by a noun in the Accusative case, and the system translated a respective noun with the Accusative case as well. However, the surface realization of the argument is different in Russian – the Russian verb requires a prepositional phrase, so the two RBMT produced an error because neither had a rule covering this discrepancy:

(2)

(src) *ovlivnit* *výsledky* *voleb*
influence results-Acc.Pl elections-Gen
'To influence results of the elections'

(ref) *повлиять* ***на*** *результаты* *выборов*
influence **on** results-Acc.Pl elections-Gen
'To influence results of the elections'

(tmt) **повлиять* *результаты* *выборов*
influence results-Acc.Pl elections-Gen
*'To influence results elections'

RBMT errors in valency are only partially related to some discrepancy in Czech and Russian. The system also make errors in cases when the valency structure of a verb in Czech and Russian was similar, like in the example below:

(3)

(src) *demokratičtí* *kritici* *hovoří* *o* *předpojatosti* *zákonů*
democratic critics speak about prejudice-**Gen**.Sg laws-Gen.Pl
'democratic critics speak about prejudice of law'

(tmt) *Демократические* *критики* *говорят* *о* *предубеждение* *законов*
democratic critics speak about prejudice-**Acc**.Sg laws-Gen.Pl
*'democratic critics speak about prejudice of law'

Those errors might be the result of an improper analysis of the source phrase or some error in the transfer or generation phases. The errors that originate from the differences between the frames in the two languages can be fixed by introducing the valency lexicon.

5 Exploiting valency information from Ruslan dictionary in machine translation

We have exploited the entries from the Ruslan lexicon described above within the TectoMT system to see if there is some improvement in the translation. In order to integrate the dictionary into the system, we have transformed the entries into the special format verb+formeme [2]. Formemes (Dušek et al., 2012) are morphosyntactic properties of the node which were created especially for the TectoMT, they contain surface valency information:

(4) **narazit n:na+4 => столкнуться n:c+7** – *to run into smb*

The list of formemes was incorporated into a system in the form of a block – FixValency.pm.[3] We evaluated the performance on the WMT test set (3000 sentences). We measured the BLEU score and manually checked the differences in the two outputs - before and after the new block was introduced. After implementing this block, some sentences with troublemaking verbs (verbs with different surface valency) were translated with a proper surface form. In examples below, (1TMT) is a test translation before applying the rules and (2TMT) after applying the rules.

In the following example, a Czech verb *využívat* – 'use' governs a complement in the Dative case, and in the baseline (1TMT) system, the complement received the same formeme as a default. However, in Russian the Accusative case should be used instead. This discrepancy was covered by the Ruslan entry (využívat + Dat -> использовать + Acc)[4] in the improved system (2TMT).

(5)

(SRC) *využívali* *obrovských* *amerických* *zakázek*
used-3Pl huge-**Gen** american-**Gen** contracts-**Gen**
' they made use of huge American contracts'

[2]In formemes, and according to the Czech tradition, cases are indicated as numbers, e.g. 4 is Accusative, 7 is Instrumental.

[3]`https://github.com/ufal/treex/blob/master/lib/Treex/Block/T2T/CS2RU/FixValency.pm`.

[4]využívat n:2 => использовать n:4 in the block FixValency.pm

(1TMT) **они использовали огромных американских заказов*
*they used huge-**Gen** american-**Gen** contracts-**Gen**
' they made use of huge American contracts'

(2TMT) *они использовали огромные американские заказы*
they used huge-**Acc** american-**Acc** contracts-**Acc**
' they made use of huge American contracts'

However, there were cases when this rule worsened the translation. In Example 6, the prepositional complement was translated properly by (1TMT) because a rule for the preposition transfer from another module[5] was applied (**n:pro+4 -> n:для+2** – n:for+Acc -> n:for+Gen). In the version with the lexicon, this rule was overridden by the rule from a new FixValency.pm module ("připravit n:pro+4" => "готовить n:про+4"). The latter verb-formeme Russian equivalent is a mistake in the Ruslan lexicon.[6]

(6)

(SRC) *v kuchyni se pro hosty připravuje čaj.*
in kitchen refl **for** guests-**Acc** prepare tea
'In the kitchen the tea for the guests is preparing'

(1TMT) *В кухне для гостей готовится чай.*
in kitchen for guests prepare-refl tea
'In the kitchen the tea **for** the guests-**Gen** is preparing'

(2TMT) **В кухне про гости готовится чай.*
*in kitchen for guests prepare-refl tea
'In the kitchen the tea **about** the guests-**Acc** is preparing'

In some sentences, both translations were incorrect due to various reasons. In Example 7, the light verb phrase *nabývá účinnosti(Gen) vs. вступит в силу (в + Acc)* – 'takes effect' is different in Czech and Russian; it should have been translated with another verb and another noun. The rule has no effect in this case, as the translation is wrong all the same.

(7)

(SRC) *zákon nabývá účinnosti 6 prosince*
law gains effect 6 December
'The law takes effect on 6 December'

(1TMT) *закон приобретать эффективности 6 декабря*
law *gains *effect-**Gen** 6 December
'The law gains effect on 6 December'

(2TMT) *закон *приобретать *эффективность 6 декабря*
law *gains *effect-**Acc** 6 December
'The law takes effect on December 6'

The above examples show that using the valency resource helps in some cases and harms in some others. Also, there was no significant influence on the BLEU score: **9.40%** without and **9.37%** with the module FixValency.pm.

[5] `https://github.com/ufal/treex/blob/master/lib/Treex/Block/T2T/CS2RU/RuleBasedFormemes.pm`

[6] As the dictionary was compiled by non-native Russian speakers, there are a few errors in the lexicon and this one illustrates how people automatically assign a surface frame from their native Czech language to the verb in Russian.

6 Manual evaluation

For such a small experiment, the BLEU score can not necessarily indicate if this valency module helped or not – we evaluated the experiment only on the reference translations with one example. We evaluated manually the cases where a valency frame was changed according to the lexicon. It was impossible to count the exact number of cases when the pattern from the lexicon was applied because mostly the valency pattern stayed the same.

We have marked a list of changes between the (1TMT) and (2TMT) outputs indicating whether the introduction of a new rule:

- lead to some improvement like in Example 5
- worsened the translation like in Example 6
- did not have any effect as both variants were incorrect – Example 7

Effect	number of differences	Percentage
improved	28	58.3 %
worsened	3	6.2%
no effect	17	35.4%
Total	48	100%

Table 1: Manual evaluation of changes after adding FixValency.pm

From the table we can see that in the majority of cases the verbal valency is improved, or it has no effect on the translation which is wrong this way or that. However, such a little fix did not bring any sufficient gain or loss when considering the automatic evaluation metric BLEU.

7 Conclusion

We described the experiment with introducing valency information into an MT system between Czech and Russian. The BLEU score showed no improvement, but the manual evaluation revealed the cases where the valency errors were fixed.

Our initial assumption that errors in valency would occur only when there is some discrepancy in Czech and Russian valency structures turned out to be false. Many words were marked as a valency error even though the Czech and Russian verbs had the same frame with the same morphological cases. This may be due to the low performance of analysis or synthesis modules of the system, when the wrong case/preposition can be used even if the valency patterns for Czech and Russian are identical. So it is crucial to improve other 'core' modules of the system to insure the proper integration of the lexicon into the translation pipeline.

8 Acknowledgment

This work has been supported by the grants FP7-ICT-2013-10-610516 (QTLeap) and LINDAT/CLARIN project No. LM2015071 of the Ministry of Education, Youth and Sports of the Czech Republic.

References

Ondřej Dušek, Zdeněk Žabokrtský, Martin Popel, Martin Majliš, Michal Novák, and David Mareček. 2012. Formemes in English-Czech Deep Syntactic MT. In *Proceedings of the Seventh Workshop on Statistical Machine Translation*, pages 267–274, Montréal, Canada. Association for Computational Linguistics.

Jan Hajic. 1987. RUSLAN: An MT System Between Closely Related Languages. In *Proceedings of the Third Conference on European Chapter of the Association for Computational Linguistics*, EACL '87, pages 113–117, Stroudsburg, PA, USA. Association for Computational Linguistics.

Karel Oliva. 1989. A parser for czech implemented in systems q. Explizite Beschreibung der Sprache und automatische Textbearbeitung, MFF UK Prague, .

Kishore Papineni, Salim Roukos, Todd Ward, and Wei jing Zhu. 2002. BLEU: a Method for Automatic Evaluation of Machine Translation. pages 311–318.

Martin Popel and Zdeněk Žabokrtský. 2009. Improving English-Czech Tectogrammatical MT. *The Prague Bulletin of Mathematical Linguistics*, (92):1–20.

Martin Popel. 2010. English-Czech Machine Translation Using TectoMT. In Jana Šafránková and Jiří Pavlů, editors, *WDS 2010 Proceedings of Contributed Papers*, pages 88–93, Praha, Czechia. Univerzita Karlova v Praze, Matfyzpress, Charles University.

P. Sgall, E. Hajicová, J. Panevová, and J. Mey. 1986. *The Meaning of the Sentence in Its Semantic and Pragmatic Aspects*. Springer.

Association for Computational Linguistics
209 N. Eighth Street
Stroudsburg, Pennsylvania 18360

CURRAN ASSOCIATES INC.
proceedings.com

ISBN 978-1-5108-3156-8
9 781510 831568